The
Poetry of
Christina
Rossetti

The
Poetry of
Christina
Rossetti

This edition published in 2019 by Arcturus Publishing Limited
26/27 Bickels Yard, 151–153 Bermondsey Street,
London SE1 3HA

AD006520UK

Printed in the UK

Contents

Introduction

Christina Georgina Rossetti was one of the finest poets of the Victorian age. Today, her reputation is largely based on her association with the Pre-Raphaelites, particularly because of her brother Dante Gabriel, but also as the writer of the carol, 'In the Bleak Mid-Winter', and her most famous poem 'Goblin Market'. However, she also wrote poems of love, fantasy and nature, verses for children and devotional poetry and prose. In the early years of the 20th century, her work faded from view, as it contained too much Victorian spirituality for modernist tastes. It remained largely unread until feminist scholars began to show interest. In the last few decades, her work has been rediscovered and has been readmitted to the Victorian canon.

Christina was born in London in December 1830, the youngest daughter of Gabriele, a poet, scholar and political refugee from Naples, and Frances Rossetti, also a scholar of Italian extraction. By all accounts, Christina was a lively, pretty child, precocious and with a vivid imagination. The children received their earliest education from their mother and all four developed artistic and literary inclinations. Maria Francesca as a writer, Dante Gabriel as a poet and painter, and William Michael as a writer and critic as well as a co-founder of the Pre-Raphaelite Brotherhood with Dante Gabriel.

Gabriele Rossetti's health collapsed in 1843, leaving him unable to work and the family in straightened circumstances. Frances, Maria and William took jobs in order to make ends meet. Dante Gabriel continued his art studies, while Christina remained at home as a companion to their ailing father. In 1845, she, too, suffered a collapse in health, regular recurrences of which led her brother William to describe her later as 'an almost constant and often a sadly smitten invalid'. During this period, Christina developed a religious devotion that would subsequently determine the course of her personal life – characterised by two failed love affairs and a self-presumed sinfulness – and colour the majority of her poetic output.

Christina began writing poetry at the age of seven, but her first commercially published work, *Goblin Market and Other Poems*, did not appear until 1862. *The Prince's Progress and Other Poems* followed in 1866 and *A Pageant and Other Poems* in 1881. She also published a number of children's books, but it was her poetry that secured her fame – much of which is included in this handsome edition.

Her poems, often filled with sadness (her father died in 1854) and marked by her deeply religious temperament, are beautiful, melancholic and austere, often deceptively simple but always written from the heart. With recurrent themes of the inconstancy of love, the vanity of earthly pleasures, individual unworthiness and the primacy of divine love, it is easy to imagine that they are reflections of her life experiences. She was also morbidly obsessed with death, perhaps looking forward to it as a release from a life of constant ill health and a final union with God when it came to an end.

In 1871, Christina was stricken by Graves' disease, which ruined her beauty and brought her close to death. When she recovered, she turned almost exclusively to religious writing. In 1891, she was diagnosed with breast cancer and died, after a long and painful illness, on 29 December 1894, in London.

A Birthday

My heart is like a singing bird
    Whose nest is in a watered shoot;
My heart is like an apple-tree
    Whose boughs are bent with thickset fruit;
My heart is like a rainbow shell
    That paddles in a halcyon sea;
My heart is gladder than all these
    Because my love is come to me.

Raise me a dais of silk and down;
    Hang it with vair and purple dyes;
Carve it in doves and pomegranates,
    And peacocks with a hundred eyes;
Work it in gold and silver grapes,
    In leaves and silver fleurs-de-lys;
Because the birthday of my life
    Is come, my love is come to me.

Twice

I took my heart in my hand
    (O my love, O my love),
I said: Let me fall or stand,
    Let me live or die,
But this once hear me speak
    (O my love, O my love);
Yet a woman's words are weak:
    You should speak, not I.

You took my heart in your hand
    With a friendly smile,
With a critical eye you scanned,
    Then set it down,
And said: It is still unripe,
    Better wait awhile;
Wait while the skylarks pipe,
    Till the corn grows brown.

As you set it down it broke, –
    Broke, but I did not wince;
I smiled at the speech you spoke,
    At your judgment that I heard:
But I have not often smiled
    Since then, nor questioned
      since,
Nor cared for corn-flowers wild,
    Nor sung with the singing bird.

I take my heart in my hand,
    O my God, O my God,

My broken heart in my hand:
    Thou hast seen, judge Thou.
My hope was written on sand,
    O my God, O my God;
Now let Thy judgment stand, —
    Yea, judge me now.

This contemned of a man,
    This marred one heedless day,
This heart take Thou to scan
    Both within and without:
Refine with fire its gold,
    Purge Thou its dross away, —
Yea, hold it in Thy hold,
    Whence none can pluck it out.

I take my heart in my hand, —
    I shall not die, but live, —
Before Thy face I stand;
    I, for Thou callest such:
All that I have I bring,
    All that I am I give,
Smile Thou and I shall sing,
    But shall not question much.

Sleeping at Last

Sleeping at last, the trouble and tumult over,
  Sleeping at last, the struggle and horror past,
Cold and white, out of sight of friend and of lover,
    Sleeping at last.

  No more a tired heart downcast or overcast,
No more pangs that wring or shifting fears that hover,
    Sleeping at last in a dreamless sleep locked fast.

Fast asleep. Singing birds in their leafy cover
   Cannot wake her, nor shake her the gusty blast.
Under the purple thyme and the purple clover
    Sleeping at last.

A Daughter of Eve

A fool I was to sleep at noon,
  And wake when night is chilly
Beneath the comfortless cold moon;
A fool to pluck my rose too soon,
  A fool to snap my lily.

My garden-plot I have not kept;
  Faded and all-forsaken,
I weep as I have never wept:
Oh it was summer when I slept,
  It's winter now I waken.

Talk what you please of future spring
  And sun-warmed sweet tomorrow: –
Stripped bare of hope and every thing,
No more to laugh, no more to sing,
  I sit alone with sorrow.

Shut Out

The door was shut. I looked between
    Its iron bars; and saw it lie,
    My garden, mine, beneath the sky,
Pied with all flowers bedewed and green:

From bough to bough the song-birds crossed,
    From flower to flower the moths and bees;
    With all its nests and stately trees
It had been mine, and it was lost.

A shadowless spirit kept the gate,
    Blank and unchanging like the grave.
    I peering thro' said: 'Let me have
Some buds to cheer my outcast state.'

He answered not. 'Or give me, then,
    But one small twig from shrub or tree;
    And bid my home remember me
Until I come to it again.'

The spirit was silent; but he took
    Mortar and stone to build a wall;
    He left no loophole great or small
Thro' which my straining eyes might look:

So now I sit here quite alone
    Blinded with tears; nor grieve for that,
    For naught is left worth looking at
Since my delightful land is gone.

A violet bed is budding near,
    Wherein a lark has made her nest:
    And good they are, but not the best;
And dear they are, but not so dear.

When I am Dead, my Dearest

When I am dead, my dearest,
　　Sing no sad songs for me;
Plant thou no roses at my head,
　　Nor shady cypress-tree:
Be the green grass above me
　　With showers and dewdrops wet;
And if thou wilt, remember,
　　And if thou wilt, forget.

I shall not see the shadows,
　　I shall not feel the rain;
I shall not hear the nightingale
　　Sing on, as if in pain:
And dreaming through the twilight
　　That doth not rise nor set,
Haply I may remember,
　　And haply may forget.

Amor Mundi

'O where are you going with your love-locks flowing,
    On the west wind blowing along this valley
        track?'
'The downhill path is easy, come with me an it
    please ye,
        We shall escape the uphill by never turning back.'

So they two went together in glowing August weather,
    The honey-breathing heather lay to their left and
        right;
And dear she was to doat on, her swift feet seemed to
    float on
        The air like soft twin pigeons too sportive to alight.

'Oh, what is that in heaven where grey cloud-flakes are
    seven,
        Where blackest clouds hang riven just at the rainy
            skirt?'
'Oh, that's a meteor sent us, a message dumb,
    portentous,
        An undeciphered solemn signal of help or hurt.'

'Oh, what is that glides quickly where velvet flowers grow
    thickly,
        Their scent comes rich and sickly?' – 'A scaled and
            hooded worm.'
'Oh, what's that in the hollow, so pale I quake to
    follow?'
        'Oh, that's a thin dead body which waits the eternal
            term.'

'Turn again, O my sweetest, – turn again, false and
    fleetest:
        This beaten way thou beatest I fear is hell's own
            track.'
'Nay, too steep for hill mounting; nay, too late for cost-
    counting:
        This downhill path is easy, but there's no turning
            back.'

Winter: My Secret

I tell my secret? No indeed, not I;
Perhaps some day, who knows?
But not today; it froze, and blows and snows,
And you're too curious: fie!
You want to hear it? well:
Only, my secret's mine, and I won't tell.

Or, after all, perhaps there's none:
Suppose there is no secret after all,
But only just my fun.
Today's a nipping day, a biting day;
In which one wants a shawl,
A veil, a cloak, and other wraps:
I cannot ope to every one who taps,
And let the draughts come whistling thro' my hall;
Come bounding and surrounding me,
Come buffeting, astounding me,
Nipping and clipping thro' my wraps and all.
I wear my mask for warmth: who ever shows
His nose to Russian snows
To be pecked at by every wind that blows?
You would not peck? I thank you for good-will,
Believe, but leave that truth untested still.

Spring's an expansive time: yet I don't trust
March with its peck of dust,
Nor April with its rainbow-crowned brief showers,
Nor even May, whose flowers
One frost may wither thro' the sunless hours.

Perhaps some languid summer day,
When drowsy birds sing less and less,
And golden fruit is ripening to excess,
If there's not too much sun nor too much cloud,
And the warm wind is neither still nor loud,
Perhaps my secret I may say,
Or you may guess.

Remember

Remember me when I am gone away,
    Gone far away into the silent land;
    When you can no more hold me by the hand,
Nor I half turn to go yet turning stay.
Remember me when no more, day by day,
    You tell me of our future that you planned:
    Only remember me; you understand
It will be late to counsel then or pray.
Yet if you should forget me for a while
    And afterwards remember, do not grieve:
    For if the darkness and corruption leave
    A vestige of the thoughts that once I had,
Better by far you should forget and smile
    Than that you should remember and be sad.

Good Friday

Am I a stone and not a sheep
    That I can stand, O Christ, beneath Thy Cross,
    To number drop by drop Thy Blood's slow loss,
And yet not weep?

Not so those women loved
    Who with exceeding grief lamented Thee;
    Not so fallen Peter weeping bitterly;
Not so the thief was moved;

Not so the Sun and Moon
    Which hid their faces in a starless sky,
    A horror of great darkness at broad noon, –
I, only I.

Yet give not o'er,
    But seek Thy sheep, true Shepherd of the flock;
Greater than Moses, turn and look once more
    And smite a rock.

From Sunset to Star Rise

Go from me, summer friends, and tarry not:
    I am no summer friend, but wintry cold,
    A silly sheep benighted from the fold,
A sluggard with a thorn-choked garden plot.
Take counsel, sever from my lot your lot,
    Dwell in your pleasant places, hoard your gold;
    Lest you with me should shiver on the wold,
Athirst and hungering on a barren spot.
For I have hedged me with a thorny hedge,
    I live alone, I look to die alone:
Yet sometimes when a wind sighs through the sedge,
    Ghosts of my buried years and friends come back,
My heart goes sighing after swallows flown
    On sometime summer's unreturning track.

Goblin Market

Morning and evening
Maids heard the goblins cry:
'Come buy our orchard fruits,
Come buy, come buy:
Apples and quinces,
Lemons and oranges,
Plump unpecked cherries,
Melons and raspberries,
Bloom-down-cheeked peaches,
Swart-headed mulberries,
Wild free-born cranberries,
Crab-apples, dewberries,
Pine-apples, blackberries,
Apricots, strawberries; —
All ripe together
In summer weather, —
Morns that pass by,
Fair eves that fly;
Come buy, come buy:
Our grapes fresh from the
    vine,
Pomegranates full and fine,
Dates and sharp bullaces,
Rare pears and greengages,
Damsons and bilberries,
Taste them and try:
Currants and gooseberries,
Bright-fire-like barberries,
Figs to fill your mouth,
Citrons from the South,

Sweet to tongue and sound to eye;
Come buy, come buy.'

Evening by evening
Among the brookside rushes,
Laura bowed her head to hear,
Lizzie veiled her blushes:
Crouching close together
In the cooling weather,
With clasping arms and cautioning lips,
With tingling cheeks and finger tips.
'Lie close,' Laura said,
Pricking up her golden head:
'We must not look at goblin men,
We must not buy their fruits:
Who knows upon what soil they fed
Their hungry thirsty roots?'
'Come buy,' call the goblins
Hobbling down the glen.
'O,' cried Lizzie, 'Laura, Laura,
You should not peep at goblin men.'
Lizzie covered up her eyes,
Covered close lest they should look;
Laura reared her glossy head,
And whispered like the restless brook:
'Look, Lizzie, look, Lizzie,
Down the glen tramp little men.
One hauls a basket,
One bears a plate,
One lugs a golden dish
Of many pounds weight.
How fair the vine must grow

Whose grapes are so luscious;
How warm the wind must blow
Thro' those fruit bushes.'
'No,' said Lizzie, 'no, no, no;
Their offers should not charm us,
Their evil gifts would harm us.'
She thrust a dimpled finger
In each ear, shut eyes and ran:
Curious Laura chose to linger
Wondering at each merchant man.
One had a cat's face,
One whisked a tail,
One tramped at a rat's pace,
One crawled like a snail,
One like a wombat prowled obtuse and furry,
One like a ratel tumbled hurry scurry.
She heard a voice like voice of doves
Cooing all together:
They sounded kind and full of loves
In the pleasant weather.

Laura stretched her gleaming neck
Like a rush-imbedded swan,
Like a lily from the beck,
Like a moonlit poplar branch,
Like a vessel at the launch
When its last restraint is gone.

Backwards up the mossy glen
Turned and trooped the goblin men,
With their shrill repeated cry,
'Come buy, come buy.'

When they reached where Laura was
They stood stock still upon the moss,
Leering at each other,
Brother with queer brother;
Signalling each other,
Brother with sly brother.
One set his basket down,
One reared his plate;
One began to weave a crown
Of tendrils, leaves, and rough nuts brown
(Men sell not such in any town);
One heaved the golden weight
Of dish and fruit to offer her:
'Come buy, come buy,' was still their cry.
Laura stared but did not stir,
Longed but had no money:
The whisk-tailed merchant bade her taste
In tones as smooth as honey,
The cat-faced purr'd,
The rat-paced spoke a word
Of welcome, and the snail-paced even was heard;
One parrot-voiced and jolly
Cried 'Pretty Goblin' still for 'Pretty Polly'; –
One whistled like a bird.

But sweet-tooth Laura spoke in haste:
'Good folk, I have no coin;
To take were to purloin:
I have no copper in my purse,
I have no silver either,
And all my gold is on the furze
That shakes in windy weather

Above the rusty heather.'
'You have much gold upon your head,'
They answered altogether:
'Buy from us with a golden curl.'
She clipped a precious golden lock,
She dropped a tear more rare than pearl,
Then sucked their fruit globes fair or red:
Sweeter than honey from the rock,
Stronger than man-rejoicing wine,
Clearer than water flowed that juice;
She never tasted such before,
How should it cloy with length of use?
She sucked and sucked and sucked the more
Fruits which that unknown orchard bore;
She sucked until her lips were sore;
Then flung the emptied rinds away,
But gathered up one kernel-stone,
And knew not was it night or day
As she turned home alone.

Lizzie met her at the gate
Full of wise upbraidings:
'Dear, you should not stay so late,
Twilight is not good for maidens;
Should not loiter in the glen
In the haunts of goblin men.
Do you not remember Jeanie,
How she met them in the moonlight,
Took their gifts both choice and many,
Ate their fruits and wore their flowers
Plucked from bowers
Where summer ripens at all hours?

But ever in the noonlight
She pined and pined away;
Sought them by night and day,
Found them no more, but dwindled and grew gray,
Then fell with the first snow,
While to this day no grass will grow
Where she lies low:
I planted daisies there a year ago
That never blow.
You should not loiter so.'
'Nay, hush,' said Laura:
'Nay, hush, my sister:
I ate and ate my fill,
Yet my mouth waters still;
Tomorrow night I will
Buy more,'
     – and kissed her.
'Have done with sorrow;
I'll bring you plums tomorrow
Fresh on their mother twigs,
Cherries worth getting;
You cannot think what figs
My teeth have met in,
What melons icy-cold
Piled on a dish of gold
Too huge for me to hold,
What peaches with a velvet nap,
Pellucid grapes without one seed:
Odorous indeed must be the mead
Whereon they grow, and pure the wave they drink
With lilies at the brink,
And sugar-sweet their sap.'

Golden head by golden head,
Like two pigeons in one nest
Folded in each other's wings,
They lay down in their curtained bed:
Like two blossoms on one stem,
Like two flakes of new-fallen snow,
Like two wands of ivory
Tipped with gold for awful kings.
Moon and stars gazed in at them,
Wind sang to them lullaby,
Lumbering owls forbore to fly,
Not a bat flapped to and fro
Round their rest:
Cheek to cheek and breast to breast
Locked together in one nest.

Early in the morning
When the first cock crowed his warning,
Neat like bees, as sweet and busy,
Laura rose with Lizzie:
Fetched in honey, milked the cows,
Aired and set to rights the house,
Kneaded cakes of whitest wheat,
Cakes for dainty mouths to eat,
Next churned butter, whipped up cream,
Fed their poultry, sat and sewed;
Talked as modest maidens should:
Lizzie with an open heart,
Laura in an absent dream,
One content, one sick in part;
One warbling for the mere bright day's delight,
One longing for the night.

At length slow evening came:
They went with pitchers to the reedy brook;
Lizzie most placid in her look,
Laura most like a leaping flame.
They drew the gurgling water from its deep;
Lizzie plucked purple and rich golden flags,
Then turning homeward said: 'The sunset flushes
Those furthest loftiest crags;
Come, Laura, not another maiden lags,
No wilful squirrel wags,
The beasts and birds are fast asleep.'
But Laura loitered still among the rushes
And said the bank was steep.

And said the hour was early still,
The dew not fallen, the wind not chill:
Listening ever, but not catching
The customary cry,
'Come buy, come buy,'
With its iterated jingle
Of sugar-baited words:
Not for all her watching
Once discerning even one goblin
Racing, whisking, tumbling, hobbling;
Let alone the herds
That used to tramp along the glen,
In groups or single,
Of brisk fruit-merchant men.
Till Lizzie urged: 'O Laura, come;
I hear the fruit-call, but I dare not look:
You should not loiter longer at this brook:
Come with me home.

The stars rise, the moon bends her arc,
Each glow-worm winks her spark,
Let us get home before the night grows dark;
For clouds may gather
Tho' this is summer weather,
Put out the lights and drench us thro';
Then if we lost our way what should we do?'

Laura turned cold as stone
To find her sister heard that cry alone,
That goblin cry,
'Come buy our fruits, come buy.'
Must she then buy no more such dainty fruit?
Must she no more such succous pasture find,
Gone deaf and blind?
Her tree of life drooped from the root:
She said not one word in her heart's sore ache;
But peering thro' the dimness, naught discerning,
Trudged home, her pitcher dripping all the way;
So crept to bed, and lay
Silent till Lizzie slept;
Then sat up in a passionate yearning,
And gnashed her teeth for balked desire, and wept
As if her heart would break.

Day after day, night after night,
Laura kept watch in vain,
In sullen silence of exceeding pain.
She never caught again the goblin cry:
'Come buy, come buy;' –
She never spied the goblin men
Hawking their fruits along the glen:

But when the noon waxed bright
Her hair grew thin and gray;
She dwindled, as the fair full moon doth turn
To swift decay, and burn
Her fire away.

One day remembering her kernel-stone
She set it by a wall that faced the south;
Dewed it with tears, hoped for a root,
Watched for a waxing shoot,
But there came none;
It never saw the sun,
It never felt the trickling moisture run:
While with sunk eyes and faded mouth
She dreamed of melons, as a traveller sees
False waves in desert drouth
With shade of leaf-crowned trees,
And burns the thirstier in the sandful breeze.

She no more swept the house,
Tended the fowls or cows,
Fetched honey, kneaded cakes of wheat,
Brought water from the brook:
But sat down listless in the chimney-nook
And would not eat.

Tender Lizzie could not bear
To watch her sister's cankerous care,
Yet not to share.
She night and morning
Caught the goblins' cry:
'Come buy our orchard fruits,

Come buy, come buy:' –
Beside the brook, along the glen,
She heard the tramp of goblin men,
The voice and stir
Poor Laura could not hear;
Longed to buy fruit to comfort her,
But feared to pay too dear.
She thought of Jeanie in her grave,
Who should have been a bride;
But who for joys brides hope to have
Fell sick and died
In her gay prime,
In earliest Winter time,
With the first glazing rime,
With the first snow-fall of crisp Winter time.

Till Laura, dwindling,
Seemed knocking at Death's door:
Then Lizzie weighed no more
Better and worse,
But put a silver penny in her purse,
Kissed Laura, crossed the heath with clumps of furze
At twilight, halted by the brook;
And for the first time in her life
Began to listen and look.

Laughed every goblin
When they spied her peeping:
Came towards her hobbling,
Flying, running, leaping,
Puffing and blowing,
Chuckling, clapping, crowing,

Clucking and gobbling,
Mopping and mowing,
Full of airs and graces,
Pulling wry faces,
Demure grimaces,
Cat-like and rat-like,
Ratel- and wombat-like,
Snail-paced in a hurry,
Parrot-voiced and whistler,
Helter skelter, hurry skurry,
Chattering like magpies,
Fluttering like pigeons,
Gliding like fishes, —
Hugged her and kissed her;
Squeezed and caressed her;
Stretched up their dishes,
Panniers and plates:
'Look at our apples
Russet and dun,
Bob at our cherries,
Bite at our peaches,
Citrons and dates,
Grapes for the asking,
Pears red with basking
Out in the sun,
Plums on their twigs;
Pluck them and suck them,
Pomegranates, figs.'

'Good folk,' said Lizzie,
Mindful of Jeanie:
'Give me much and many:" —

Held out her apron,
Tossed them her penny.
'Nay, take a seat with us,
Honor and eat with us,'
They answered grinning:
'Our feast is but beginning.
Night yet is early,
Warm and dew-pearly,
Wakeful and starry:
Such fruits as these
No man can carry;
Half their bloom would fly,
Half their dew would dry,
Half their flavor would pass by.
Sit down and feast with us,
Be welcome guest with us,
Cheer you and rest with us.'
'Thank you,' said Lizzie; 'but one waits
At home alone for me:
So, without further parleying,
If you will not sell me any
Of your fruits tho' much and many,
Give me back my silver penny
I tossed you for a fee.' —
They began to scratch their pates,
No longer wagging, purring,
But visibly demurring,
Grunting and snarling.
One called her proud,
Cross-grained, uncivil;
Their tones waxed loud,
Their looks were evil.

Lashing their tails
They trod and hustled her,
Elbowed and jostled her,
Clawed with their nails,
Barking, mewing, hissing, mocking,
Tore her gown and soiled her stocking,
Twitched her hair out by the roots,
Stamped upon her tender feet,
Held her hands and squeezed their fruits
Against her mouth to make her eat.

White and golden Lizzie stood,
Like a lily in a flood, —
Like a rock of blue-veined stone
Lashed by tides obstreperously, —
Like a beacon left alone
In a hoary roaring sea,
Sending up a golden fire, —
Like a fruit-crowned orange-tree
White with blossoms honey-sweet
Sore beset by wasp and bee, —
Like a royal virgin town
Topped with gilded dome and spire
Close beleaguered by a fleet
Mad to tug her standard down.

One may lead a horse to water,
Twenty cannot make him drink.
Tho' the goblins cuffed and caught her,
Coaxed and fought her,
Bullied and besought her,
Scratched her, pinched her black as ink,

Kicked and knocked her,
Mauled and mocked her,
Lizzie uttered not a word;
Would not open lip from lip
Lest they should cram a mouthful in:
But laughed in heart to feel the drip
Of juice that syrupped all her face,
And lodged in dimples of her chin,
And streaked her neck which quaked like curd.
At last the evil people,
Worn out by her resistance,
Flung back her penny, kicked their fruit
Along whichever road they took,
Not leaving root or stone or shoot.
Some writhed into the ground,
Some dived into the brook
With ring and ripple,
Some scudded on the gale without a sound,
Some vanished in the distance.

In a smart, ache, tingle,
Lizzie went her way;
Knew not was it night or day;
Sprang up the bank, tore thro' the furze,
Threaded copse and dingle,
And heard her penny jingle
Bouncing in her purse,
Its bounce was music to her ear.
She ran and ran
As if she feared some goblin man
Dogged her with gibe or curse
Or something worse:

But not one goblin skurried after,
Nor was she pricked by fear;
The kind heart made her windy-paced
That urged her home quite out of breath with haste
And inward laughter.

She cried 'Laura,' up the garden,
'Did you miss me?
Come and kiss me.
Never mind my bruises,
Hug me, kiss me, suck my juices
Squeezed from goblin fruits for you,
Goblin pulp and goblin dew.
Eat me, drink me, love me;
Laura, make much of me:
For your sake I have braved the glen
And had to do with goblin merchant men.'

Laura started from her chair,
Flung her arms up in the air,
Clutched her hair:
'Lizzie, Lizzie, have you tasted
For my sake the fruit forbidden?
Must your light like mine be hidden,
Your young life like mine be wasted,
Undone in mine undoing
And ruined in my ruin,
Thirsty, cankered, goblin-ridden?' –
She clung about her sister,
Kissed and kissed and kissed her:
Tears once again
Refreshed her shrunken eyes,

Dropping like rain
After long sultry drouth;
Shaking with aguish fear, and pain,
She kissed and kissed her with a hungry mouth.

Her lips began to scorch,
That juice was wormwood to her tongue,
She loathed the feast:
Writhing as one possessed she leaped and sung,
Rent all her robe, and wrung
Her hands in lamentable haste,
And beat her breast.
Her locks streamed like the torch
Borne by a racer at full speed,
Or like the mane of horses in their flight,
Or like an eagle when she stems the light
Straight toward the sun,
Or like a caged thing freed,
Or like a flying flag when armies run.

Swift fire spread thro' her veins, knocked at her heart,
Met the fire smouldering there
And overbore its lesser flame;
She gorged on bitterness without a name:
Ah! fool, to choose such part
Of soul-consuming care!
Sense failed in the mortal strife:
Like the watch-tower of a town
Which an earthquake shatters down,
Like a lightning-stricken mast,
Like a wind-uprooted tree
Spun about,

Like a foam-topped waterspout
Cast down headlong in the sea,
She fell at last;
Pleasure past and anguish past,
Is it death or is it life?

Life out of death.
That night long Lizzie watched by her,
Counted her pulse's flagging stir,
Felt for her breath,
Held water to her lips, and cooled her face
With tears and fanning leaves:
But when the first birds chirped about their eaves,
And early reapers plodded to the place
Of golden sheaves,
And dew-wet grass
Bowed in the morning winds so brisk to pass,
And new buds with new day
Opened of cup-like lilies on the stream,
Laura awoke as from a dream,
Laughed in the innocent old way,
Hugged Lizzie but not twice or thrice;
Her gleaming locks showed not one thread of gray,
Her breath was sweet as May,
And light danced in her eyes.

Days, weeks, months, years
Afterwards, when both were wives
With children of their own;
Their mother-hearts beset with fears,
Their lives bound up in tender lives;
Laura would call the little ones

And tell them of her early prime,
Those pleasant days long gone
Of not-returning time:
Would talk about the haunted glen,
The wicked, quaint fruit-merchant men,
Their fruits like honey to the throat,
But poison in the blood;
(Men sell not such in any town;)
Would tell them how her sister stood
In deadly peril to do her good,
And win the fiery antidote:
Then joining hands to little hands
Would bid them cling together,
'For there is no friend like a sister,
In calm or stormy weather,
To cheer one on the tedious way,
To fetch one if one goes astray,
To lift one if one totters down,
To strengthen whilst one stands.'

The Thread of Life

1.

The irresponsive silence of the land,
    The irresponsive sounding of the sea,
    Speak both one message of one sense to me: —
Aloof, aloof, we stand aloof, so stand
Thou too aloof bound with the flawless band
    Of inner solitude; we bind not thee;
    But who from thy self-chain shall set thee free?
What heart shall touch thy heart? what hand thy
    hand? —
And I am sometimes proud and sometimes meek,
    And sometimes I remember days of old
When fellowship seemed not so far to seek
    And all the world and I seemed much less cold,
    And at the rainbow's foot lay surely gold,
And hope felt strong and life itself not weak.

2.

Thus am I mine own prison. Everything
    Around me free and sunny and at ease:
    Or if in shadow, in a shade of trees
Which the sun kisses, where the gay birds sing
And where all winds make various murmuring;
    Where bees are found, with honey for the bees;
    Where sounds are music, and where silences
Are music of an unlike fashioning.
Then gaze I at the merrymaking crew,
    And smile a moment and a moment sigh
Thinking: Why can I not rejoice with you?
    But soon I put the foolish fancy by:

I am not what I have nor what I do;
    But what I was I am, I am even I.

3.

Therefore myself is that one only thing
    I hold to use or waste, to keep or give;
    My sole possession every day I live,
And still mine own despite Time's winnowing.
Ever mine own, while moons and seasons bring
    From crudeness ripeness mellow and sanative;
    Ever mine own, till Death shall ply his sieve;
And still mine own, when saints break grave and sing.
And this myself as king unto my King
    I give, to Him Who gave Himself for me;
Who gives Himself to me, and bids me sing
    A sweet new song of His redeemed set free;
He bids me sing: O death, where is thy sting?
    And sing: O grave, where is thy victory?

She Sat and Sang Alway

She sat and sang alway
    By the green margin of a stream,
Watching the fishes leap and play
    Beneath the glad sunbeam.

I sat and wept alway
    Beneath the moon's most shadowy beam,
Watching the blossoms of the May
    Weep leaves into the stream.

I wept for memory;
    She sang for hope that is so fair:
My tears were swallowed by the sea;
    Her songs died on the air.

Sound Sleep

Some are laughing, some are weeping;
She is sleeping, only sleeping.
Round her rest wild flowers are creeping;
There the wind is heaping, heaping
Sweetest sweets of Summer's keeping,
By the cornfields ripe for reaping.

There are lilies, and there blushes
The deep rose, and there the thrushes
Sing till latest sunlight flushes
In the west; a fresh wind brushes
Thro' the leaves while evening hushes.

There by day the lark is singing
And the grass and weeds are springing:
There by night the bat is winging;
There forever winds are bringing
Far-off chimes of church-bells ringing.

Night and morning, noon and even,
Their sound fills her dreams with Heaven:
The long strife at length is striven:
Till her grave-bands shall be riven,
Such is the good portion given
To her soul at rest and shriven.

In an Artist's Studio

One face looks out from all his canvases,
One selfsame figure sits or walks or leans:
We found her hidden just behind those screens,
That mirror gave back all her loveliness.
A queen in opal or in ruby dress,
A nameless girl in freshest summer-greens,
A saint, an angel; — every canvas means
The same one meaning, neither more or less.
He feeds upon her face by day and night,
And she with true kind eyes looks back on him
Fair as the moon and joyful as the light:
Not wan with waiting, not with sorrow dim;
Not as she is, but was when hope shone bright;
Not as she is, but as she fills his dream.

A Christmas Carol

In the bleak mid-winter
    Frosty wind made moan,
Earth stood hard as iron,
    Water like a stone;
Snow had fallen, snow on snow,
    Snow on snow,
In the bleak mid-winter
    Long ago.

Our God, Heaven cannot hold Him
    Nor earth sustain;
Heaven and earth shall flee away
    When He comes to reign:
In the bleak mid-winter
    A stable-place sufficed
The Lord God Almighty
    Jesus Christ.

Enough for Him whom cherubim
    Worship night and day,
A breastful of milk
    And a mangerful of hay;
Enough for Him whom angels
    Fall down before,
The ox and ass and camel
    Which adore.

Angels and archangels
    May have gathered there,
Cherubim and seraphim

Throng'd the air,
But only His mother
    In her maiden bliss
Worshipped her Beloved
    With a kiss.

What can I give Him,
    Poor as I am?
If I were a shepherd
    I would bring a lamb,
If I were a wise man
    I would do my part, —
Yet what I can I give Him,
    Give my heart.

A Song of Flight

While we slumber and sleep,
The sun leaps up from the deep,
 — Daylight born at the leap! —
Rapid, dominant, free,
Athirst to bathe in the uttermost sea.

While we linger at play
 — If the year would stand at May! —
Winds are up and away,
Over land, over sea,
To their goal, wherever their goal may be.

It is time to arise,
To race for the promised prize;
 — The Sun flies, the Wind flies, —
We are strong, we are free,
And home lies beyond the stars and the sea.

A Pause of Thought

I looked for that which is not, nor can be,
    And hope deferred made my heart sick in truth
    But years must pass before a hope of youth
      Is resigned utterly.

I watched and waited with a steadfast will:
    And though the object seemed to flee away
    That I so longed for, ever day by day
      I watched and waited still.

Sometimes I said: This thing shall be no more;
    My expectation wearies and shall cease;
    I will resign it now and be at peace:
      Yet never gave it o'er.

Sometimes I said: It is an empty name
    I long for; to a name why should I give
    The peace of all the days I have to live? —
      Yet gave it all the same.

Alas, thou foolish one! alike unfit
    For healthy joy and salutary pain:
    Thou knowest the chase useless, and again
      Turnest to follow it.

Buds and Babies

A million buds are born that never blow,
    That sweet with promise lift a pretty head
    To blush and wither on a barren bed
      And leave no fruit to show.

Sweet, unfulfilled. Yet have I understood
    One joy, by their fragility made plain:
    Nothing was ever beautiful in vain,
      Or all in vain was good.

Maude Clare

Out of the church she followed them
    With a lofty step and mien:
His bride was like a village maid,
    Maude Clare was like a queen.

'Son Thomas,' his lady mother said,
    With smiles, almost with tears:
'May Nell and you but live as true
    As we have done for years;

'Your father thirty years ago
    Had just your tale to tell;
But he was not so pale as you,
    Nor I so pale as Nell.'

My lord was pale with inward strife,
    And Nell was pale with pride;
My lord gazed long on pale Maude Clare
    Or ever he kissed the bride.

'Lo, I have brought my gift, my lord,
    Have brought my gift,' she said:
'To bless the hearth, to bless the board,
    To bless the marriage-bed.

'Here's my half of the golden chain
    You wore about your neck,
That day we waded ankle-deep
    For lilies in the beck:

'Here's my half of the faded leaves
    We plucked from budding bough,
With feet amongst the lily-leaves, –
    The lilies are budding now.'

He strove to match her scorn with scorn,
    He faltered in his place:
'Lady,' he said, – 'Maude Clare,' he said, –
    'Maude Clare': – and hid his face.

She turned to Nell: 'My Lady Nell,
    I have a gift for you;
Though, were it fruit, the bloom were gone,
    Or, were it flowers, the dew.

'Take my share of a fickle heart,
    Mine of a paltry love:
Take it or leave it as you will,
    I wash my hands thereof.'

'And what you leave,' said Nell, 'I'll take,
    And what you spurn, I'll wear;
For he's my lord for better and worse,
    And him I love, Maude Clare.

'Yea, tho' you're taller by the head,
    More wise, and much more fair;
I'll love him till he loves me best,
    Me best of all, Maude Clare.'

The World

By day she woos me, soft, exceeding fair:
But all night as the moon so changeth she;
Loathsome and foul with hideous leprosy
And subtle serpents gliding in her hair.
By day she woos me to the outer air,
Ripe fruits, sweet flowers, and full satiety:
But thro' the night, a beast she grins at me,
A very monster void of love and prayer.
By day she stands a lie: by night she stands
In all the naked horror of the truth
With pushing horns and clawed and clutching hands.
Is this a friend indeed; that I should sell
My soul to her, give her my life and youth,
Till my feet, cloven too, take hold on hell?

Dream Land

Where sunless rivers weep
Their waves into the deep,
She sleeps a charmed sleep:
    Awake her not.
Led by a single star,
She came from very far
To seek where shadows are
    Her pleasant lot.

She left the rosy morn,
She left the fields of corn,
For twilight cold and lorn
    And water springs.
Thro' sleep, as thro' a veil,
She sees the sky look pale,
And hears the nightingale
    That sadly sings.

Rest, rest, a perfect rest
Shed over brow and breast;
Her face is toward the west,
    The purple land.
She cannot see the grain
Ripening on hill and plain;
She cannot feel the rain
    Upon her hand.

Rest, rest, for evermore
Upon a mossy shore;
Rest, rest at the heart's core

Till time shall cease:
Sleep that no pain shall wake;
Night that no morn shall break,
Till joy shall overtake
Her perfect peace.

Mariana

Not for me marring or making,
Not for me giving or taking;
    I love my Love and he loves not me,
I love my Love and my heart is breaking.

Sweet is Spring in its lovely showing,
Sweet the violet veiled in blowing,
    Sweet it is to love and be loved;
Ah, sweet knowledge beyond my knowing!

Who sighs for love sighs but for pleasure,
Who wastes for love hoards up a treasure;
    Sweet to be loved and take no count,
Sweet it is to love without measure.

Sweet my Love whom I loved to try for,
Sweet my Love whom I love and sigh for,
    Will you once love me and sigh for me,
You my Love whom I love and die for?

Mother Country

Oh what is that country
    And where can it be,
Not mine own country,
    But dearer far to me?
Yet mine own country,
    If I one day may see
Its spices and cedars,
    Its gold and ivory.

As I lie dreaming
    It rises, that land;
There rises before me
    Its green golden strand,
With the bowing cedars
    And the shining sand;
It sparkles and flashes
    Like a shaken brand.

Do angels lean nearer
    While I lie and long?
I see their soft plumage
    And catch their windy song,
Like the rise of a high tide
    Sweeping full and strong;
I mark the outskirts
    Of their reverend throng.

Oh what is a king here,
    Or what is a boor?
Here all starve together,

All dwarfed and poor;
Here Death's hand knocketh
    At door after door,
He thins the dancers
    From the festal floor.

Oh what is a handmaid,
    Or what is a queen?
All must lie down together
    Where the turf is green,
The foulest face hidden,
    The fairest not seen;
Gone as if never
    They had breathed or been.

Gone from sweet sunshine
    Underneath the sod,
Turned from warm flesh and blood
    To senseless clod;
Gone as if never
    They had toiled or trod,
Gone out of sight of all
    Except our God.

Shut into silence
    From the accustomed song
Shut into solitude
    From all earth's throng,
Run down tho' swift of foot,
    Thrust down tho' strong;
Life made an end of
    Seemed it short or long.

Life made an end of,
        Life but just begun,
Life finished yesterday,
        Its last sand run;
Life new-born with the morrow
        Fresh as the sun:
While done is done for ever;
        Undone, undone.

And if that life is life,
        This is but a breath,
The passage of a dream
        And the shadow of death;
But a vain shadow
        If one considereth;
Vanity of vanities,
        As the Preacher saith.

Mirage

The hope I dreamed of was a dream,
    Was but a dream; and now I wake
Exceeding comfortless, and worn, and old,
    For a dream's sake.

I hang my harp upon a tree,
    A weeping willow in a lake;
I hang my silenced harp there, wrung and snapt
    For a dream's sake.

Lie still, lie still, my breaking heart;
    My silent heart, lie still and break:
Life, and the world, and mine own self, are changed
    For a dream's sake.

Wife to Husband

Pardon the faults in me,
    For the love of years ago:
        Good bye.
I must drift across the sea,
    I must sink into the snow,
        I must die.

You can bask in this sun,
    You can drink wine, and eat:
        Good bye.
I must gird myself and run,
    Tho' with unready feet:
        I must die.

Blank sea to sail upon,
    Cold bed to sleep in:
        Good bye.
While you clasp, I must be gone
    For all your weeping:
        I must die.

A kiss for one friend,
    And a word for two, −
        Good bye: −
A lock that you must send,
    A kindness you must do:
        I must die.

Not a word for you,
    Not a lock or kiss,
       Good bye.
We, one, must part in two:
    Verily death is this:
       I must die.

A Dirge

Why were you born when the snow was falling?
You should have come to the cuckoo's calling,
Or when grapes are green in the cluster,
Or, at least, when lithe swallows muster
    For their far off flying
    From summer dying.

Why did you die when the lambs were cropping?
You should have died at the apples' dropping,
When the grasshopper comes to trouble,
And the wheat-fields are sodden stubble,
    And all winds go sighing
    For sweet things dying.

Love From the North

I had a love in soft south land,
    Beloved thro' April far in May;
He waited on my lightest breath,
    And never dared to say me nay.

He saddened if my cheer was sad,
    But gay he grew if I was gay;
We never differed on a hair,
    My yes his yes, my nay his nay.

The wedding hour was come, the aisles
    Were flushed with sun and flowers that day;
I pacing balanced in my thoughts,
    'It's quite too late to think of nay.' —

My bridegroom answered in his turn,
    Myself had almost answered 'yea:'
When thro' the flashing nave I heard.
    A struggle and resounding 'nay.'

Bridemaids and bridegroom shrank in fear,
    But I stood high who stood at bay:
'And if I answer yea, fair Sir,
    What man art thou to bar with nay?'

He was a strong man from the north,
    Light-locked, with eyes of dangerous gray:
'Put yea by for another time
    In which I will not say thee nay.'

He took me in his strong white arms,
    He bore me on his horse away
O'er crag, morass, and hair-breadth pass,
    But never asked me yea or nay.

He made me fast with book and bell,
    With links of love he makes me stay;
Till now I've neither heart nor power
    Nor will nor wish to say him nay.

A Smile and a Sigh

A smile because the nights are short!
    And every morning brings such pleasure
Of sweet love-making, harmless sport:
      Love that makes and finds its treasure;
      Love, treasure without measure.

A sigh because the days are long!
    Long, long these days that pass in sighing,
A burden saddens every song:
      While time lags which should be flying,
      We live who would be dying.

Paradise

Once in a dream I saw the flowers
    That bud and bloom in Paradise;
    More fair they are than waking eyes
Have seen in all this world of ours.
And faint the perfume-bearing rose,
    And faint the lily on its stem,
And faint the perfect violet
    Compared with them.

I heard the songs of Paradise:
    Each bird sat singing in his place;
    A tender song so full of grace
It soared like incense to the skies.
Each bird sat singing to his mate
    Soft-cooing notes among the trees:
The nightingale herself were cold
    To such as these.

I saw the fourfold River flow,
    And deep it was, with golden sand;
    It flowed between a mossy land
With murmured music grave and low.
It hath refreshment for all thirst,
    For fainting spirits strength and rest;
Earth holds not such a draught as this
    From east to west.

The Tree of Life stood budding there,
    Abundant with its twelvefold fruits;
    Eternal sap sustains its roots,

Its shadowing branches fill the air.
Its leaves are healing for the world,
    Its fruit the hungry world can feed,
Sweeter than honey to the taste,
        And balm indeed.

I saw the gate called Beautiful;
    And looked, but scarce could look within;
    I saw the golden streets begin,
And outskirts of the glassy pool.
Oh harps, oh crowns of plenteous stars,
    Oh green palm branches many-leaved —
Eye hath not seen, nor ear hath heard,
        Nor heart conceived.

I hope to see these things again,
    But not as once in dreams by night;
    To see them with my very sight,
And touch and handle and attain:
To have all Heaven beneath my feet
    For narrow way that once they trod;
To have my part with all the saints,
        And with my God.

Mirrors of Life and Death

The mystery of Life, the mystery
Of Death, I see
Darkly as in a glass;
Their shadows pass,
And talk with me.

As the flush of a Morning Sky,
As a Morning Sky colourless —
Each yields its measure of light
To a wet world or a dry;
Each fares thro' day to night
With equal pace,
And then each one
Is done.

As the Sun with glory and grace
In his face,
Benignantly hot,
Graciously radiant and keen,
Ready to rise and to run, —
Not without spot,
Not even the Sun.

As the Moon
On the wax, on the wane,
With night for her noon;
Vanishing soon,
To appear again.

As Roses that droop
Half warm, half chill, in the languid May,
And breathe out a scent
Sweet and faint;
Till the wind gives one swoop
To scatter their beauty away.

As Lilies a multitude,
One dipping, one rising, one sinking,
On rippling waters, clear blue
And pure for their drinking;
One new dead, and one opened anew,
And all good.

As a cankered pale Flower,
With death for a dower,
Each hour of its life half dead;
With death for a crown
Weighing down
Its head.

As an Eagle, half strength and half grace,
Most potent to face
Unwinking the splendor of light;
Harrying the East and the West,
Soaring aloft from our sight;
Yet one day or one night dropped to rest,
On the low common earth
Of his birth.

As a Dove,
Not alone,

In a world of her own
Full of fluttering soft noises
And tender sweet voices
Of love.

As a Mouse
Keeping house
In the fork of a tree,
With nuts in a crevice,
And an acorn or two;
What cares he
For blossoming boughs,
Or the song-singing bevies
Of birds in their glee,
Scarlet, or golden, or blue?

As a Mole grubbing underground;
When it comes to the light
It grubs its way back again,
Feeling no bias of fur
To hamper it in its stir,
Scant of pleasure and pain,
Sinking itself out of sight
Without sound.

As Waters that drop and drop,
Weariness without end,
That drop and never stop,
Wear that nothing can mend,
Till one day they drop –
Stop –

And there's an end,
And matters mend.

As Trees, beneath whose skin
We mark not the sap begin
To swell and rise,
Till the whole bursts out in green:
We mark the falling leaves
When the wide world grieves
And sighs.

As a Forest on fire,
Where maddened creatures desire
Wet mud or wings
Beyond all those things
Which could assuage desire
On this side the flaming fire.

As Wind with a sob and sigh
To which there comes no reply
But a rustle and shiver
From rushes of the river;
As Wind with a desolate moan,
Moaning on alone.

As a Desert all sand,
Blank, neither water nor land
For solace, or dwelling, or culture,
Where the storms and the wild creatures howl;
Given over to lion and vulture,
To ostrich, and jackal, and owl:
Yet somewhere an oasis lies;

There waters arise
To nourish one seedling of balm,
Perhaps, or one palm.

As the Sea,
Murmuring, shifting, swaying;
One time sunnily playing,
One time wrecking and slaying;
In whichever mood it be,
Worst or best,
Never at rest.

As still Waters and deep,
As shallow Waters that brawl,
As rapid Waters that leap
To their fall.

As Music, as Colour, as Shape,
Keys of rapture and pain
Turning in vain
In a lock which turns not again,
While breaths and moments escape.

As Spring, all bloom and desire;
As Summer, all gift and fire;
As Autumn, a dying glow;
As Winter, with nought to show:

Winter which lays its dead all out of sight,
All clothed in white,
All waiting for the long-awaited light.

He and She

'Should one of us remember,
  And one of us forget,
I wish I knew what each will do —
  But who can tell as yet?'

'Should one of us remember,
  And one of us forget,
I promise you what I will do —
And I'm content to wait for you,
  And not be sure as yet.'

Maiden May

Maiden May sat in her bower,
In her blush rose bower in flower,
    Sweet of scent;
Sat and dreamed away an hour,
    Half content, half uncontent.

'Why should rose blossoms be born,
Tender blossoms, on a thorn
    Tho' so sweet?
Never a thorn besets the corn
    Scentless in its strength complete.

'Why are roses all so frail,
At the mercy of the gale,
    Of a breath?
Yet so sweet and perfect pale,
    Still so sweet in life and death.'

Maiden May sat in her bower,
In her blush rose bower in flower,
    Where a linnet
Made one bristling branch the tower
    For her nest and young ones in it.

'Gay and clear the linnet trills;
Yet the skylark only, thrills
    Heaven and earth
When he breasts the height, and fills
    Height and depth with song and mirth.

'Nightingales which yield to night
Solitary strange delight,
        Reign alone:
But the lark for all his height
        Fills no solitary throne;

'While he sings, a hundred sing;
Wing their flight below his wing
        Yet in flight;
Each a lovely joyful thing
        To the measure of its delight.

'Why then should a lark be reckoned
One alone, without a second
        Near his throne?
He in skyward flight unslackened,
        In his music, not alone.'

Maiden May sat in her bower;
Her own face was like a flower
        Of the prime,
Half in sunshine, half in shower,
        In the year's most tender time.

Her own thoughts in silent song
Musically flowed along,
        Wise, unwise,
Wistful, wondering, weak or strong:
        As brook shallows sink or rise.

Other thoughts another day,
Maiden May, will surge and sway
        Round your heart;
Wake, and plead, and turn at bay,
        Wisdom part, and folly part.

Time not far remote will borrow
Other joys, another sorrow,
        All for you;
Not to-day, and yet to-morrow
        Reasoning false and reasoning true.

Wherefore greatest? Wherefore least?
Hearts that starve and hearts that feast?
        You and I?
Stammering Oracles have ceased,
        And the whole earth stands at 'why?'

Underneath all things that be
Lies an unsolved mystery;
        Over all
Spreads a veil impenetrably,
        Spreads a dense unlifted pall.

Mystery of mysteries:
This creation hears and sees
        High and low —
Vanity of vanities:
        This we test and this we know.

Maiden May, the days of flowering
Nurse you now in sweet embowering,
    Sunny days;
Bright with rainbows all the showering,
    Bright with blossoms all the ways.

Close the inlet of your bower,
Close it close with thorn and flower,
    Maiden May;
Lengthen out the shortening hour, –
    Morrows are not as today.

Stay today which wanes too soon,
Stay the sun and stay the moon,
    Stay your youth;
Bask you in the actual noon,
    Rest you in the present truth.

Let today suffice today:
For itself tomorrow may
    Fetch its loss;
Aim and stumble, say its say,
    Watch and pray and bear its cross.

Tempus Fugit

Lovely Spring,
A brief sweet thing,
Is swift on the wing;
Gracious Summer,
A slow sweet comer,
Hastens past;
Autumn while sweet
Is all incomplete
With a moaning blast, —
Nothing can last,
Can be cleaved unto,
Can be dwelt upon;
It is hurried thro',
It is come and gone,
Undone it cannot be done,
It is ever to do,
Ever old, ever new,
Ever waxing old
And lapsing to Winter cold.

Hollow-Sounding and Mysterious

There's no replying
To the Wind's sighing,
Telling, foretelling,
Dying, undying,
Dwindling and swelling,
Complaining, droning,
Whistling and moaning,
Ever beginning,
Ending, repeating,
Hinting and dinning,
Lagging and fleeting —
We've no replying
Living or dying
To the Wind's sighing.

What are you telling,
Variable Wind-tone?
What would be teaching,
O sinking, swelling,
Desolate Wind-moan?
Ever for ever
Teaching and preaching,
Never, ah never
Making us wiser —
The earliest riser
Catches no meaning,
The last who hearkens
Garners no gleaning
Of wisdom's treasure,
While the world darkens: —

Living or dying,
In pain, in pleasure,
We've no replying
To wordless flying
Wind's sighing.

Life and Death

Life is not sweet. One day it will be sweet
      To shut our eyes and die:
Nor feel the wild flowers blow, nor birds dart by
      With flitting butterfly,
Nor grass grow long above our heads and feet,
Nor hear the happy lark that soars sky high,
Nor sigh that spring is fleet and summer fleet,
      Nor mark the waxing wheat,
Nor know who sits in our accustomed seat.

Life is not good. One day it will be good
      To die, then live again;
To sleep meanwhile: so not to feel the wane
Of shrunk leaves dropping in the wood,
Nor hear the foamy lashing of the main,
Nor mark the blackened bean-fields, nor where stood
      Rich ranks of golden grain,
Only dead refuse stubble clothe the plain:
Asleep from risk, asleep from pain.

Eve

'While I sit at the door,
Sick to gaze within,
Mine eye weepeth sore
For sorrow and sin:
As a tree my sin stands
To darken all lands;
Death is the fruit it bore.

'How have Eden bowers grown
Without Adam to bend them!
How have Eden flowers blown,
Squandering their sweet breath,
Without me to tend them!
The Tree of Life was ours,
Tree twelvefold-fruited,
Most lofty tree that flowers,
Most deeply rooted:
I chose the Tree of Death.

'Hadst thou but said me nay,
Adam, my brother,
I might have pined away;
I, but none other:
God might have let thee stay
Safe in our garden,
By putting me away
Beyond all pardon.

'I, Eve, sad mother
Of all who must live,
I, not another,
Plucked bitterest fruit to give
My friend, husband, lover; —
O wanton eyes run over;
Who but I should grieve? —
Cain hath slain his brother:
Of all who must die mother,
Miserable Eve!'

Thus she sat weeping,
Thus Eve our mother,
Where one lay sleeping
Slain by his brother.
Greatest and least
Each piteous beast
To hear her voice
Forgot his joys
And set aside his feast.

The mouse paused in his walk
And dropped his wheaten stalk;
Grave cattle wagged their heads
In rumination;
The eagle gave a cry
From his cloud station;
Larks on thyme beds
Forbore to mount or sing;
Bees drooped upon the wing;
The raven perched on high
Forgot his ration;

The conies in their rock,
A feeble nation,
Quaked sympathetical;
The mocking-bird left off to mock;
Huge camels knelt as if
In deprecation;
The kind hart's tears were falling;
Chattered the wistful stork;
Dove-voices with a dying fall
Cooed desolation,
Answering grief by grief.

Only the serpent in the dust,
Wriggling and crawling,
Grinned an evil grin, and thrust
His tongue out with its fork.

One Day

I will tell you when they met:
In the limpid days of Spring;
Elder boughs were budding yet,
Oaken boughs looked wintry still,
But primrose and veined violet
In the mossful turf were set,
While meeting birds made haste to sing
And build with right good will.

I will tell you when they parted:
When plenteous Autumn sheaves were brown,
Then they parted heavy-hearted;
The full rejoicing sun looked down
As grand as in the days before;
Only they had lost a crown;
Only to them those days of yore
Could come back nevermore.

When shall they meet? I cannot tell,
Indeed, when they shall meet again,
Except some day in Paradise:
For this they wait, one waits in pain.
Beyond the sea of death love lies
Forever, yesterday, today;
Angels shall ask them, 'Is it well?'
And they shall answer, 'Yea.'

I Wish I Could Remember That First Day

Era già l'ora che volge il desio. — Dante

Ricorro al tempo ch'io vi vidi prima. — Petrarca

I wish I could remember that first day,
First hour, first moment of your meeting me,
If bright or dim the season, it might be
Summer or Winter for aught I can say;
So unrecorded did it slip away,
So blind was I to see and to foresee,
So dull to mark the budding of my tree
That would not blossom yet for many a May.
If only I could recollect it, such
A day of days! I let it come and go
As traceless as a thaw of bygone snow;
It seemed to mean so little, meant so much;
If only now I could recall that touch,
First touch of hand in hand – Did one but know!

By the Sea

Why does the sea moan evermore?
    Shut out from heaven it makes its moan.
It frets against the boundary shore;
    All earth's full rivers cannot fill
    The sea, that drinking thirsteth still.

Sheer miracles of loveliness
    Lie hid in its unlooked-on bed:
Anemones, salt, passionless,
    Blow flower-like; just enough alive
    To blow and multiply and thrive.

Shells quaint with curve, or spot, or spike,
    Encrusted live things argus-eyed,
All fair alike, yet all unlike,
    Are born without a pang, and die
    Without a pang, – and so pass by.

A Bride Song

Thro' the vales to my love!
　　To the happy small nest of home
Green from basement to roof;
　　Where the honey-bees come
To the window-sill flowers,
　　And dive from above,
Safe from the spider that weaves
　　Her warp and her woof
In some outermost leaves.

Thro' the vales to my love!
　　In sweet April hours
　　All rainbows and showers,
While dove answers dove, –
　　In beautiful May,
When the orchards are tender
　　And frothing with flowers, –
　　In opulent June,
When the wheat stands up slender
　　By sweet-smelling hay,
And half the sun's splendour
　　Descends to the moon.

Thro' the vales to my love!
　　Where the turf is so soft to the feet,
　　And the thyme makes it sweet,
And the stately foxglove
　　Hangs silent its exquisite bells;
　　And where water wells
The greenness grows greener,

And bulrushes stand
Round a lily to screen her.

Nevertheless, if this land,
    Like a garden to smell and to sight,
Were turned to a desert of sand,
    Stripped bare of delight,
    All its best gone to worst,
For my feet no repose,
    No water to comfort my thirst,
And heaven like a furnace above, —
    The desert would be
    As gushing of waters to me,
The wilderness be as a rose,
    If it led me to thee,
    O my love!

Autumn Violets

Keep love for youth, and violets for the spring:
    Or if these bloom when worn-out autumn grieves,
    Let them lie hid in double shade of leaves,
Their own, and others dropped down withering;
For violets suit when home birds build and sing,
    Not when the outbound bird a passage cleaves;
    Not with dry stubble of mown harvest sheaves,
But when the green world buds to blossoming.
Keep violets for the spring, and love for youth,
    Love that should dwell with beauty, mirth, and hope:
      Or if a later sadder love be born,
    Let this not look for grace beyond its scope,
But give itself, nor plead for answering truth –
    A grateful Ruth tho' gleaning scanty corn.

Under the Rose

(also known as 'The iniquity of the Fathers Upon the Children')

Oh the rose of keenest thorn!
One hidden summer morn
Under the rose I was born.

I do not guess his name
Who wrought my Mother's shame,
And gave me life forlorn,
But my Mother, Mother, Mother,
I know her from all other.
My Mother pale and mild,
Fair as ever was seen,
She was but scarce sixteen,
Little more than a child,
When I was born
To work her scorn.
With secret bitter throes,
In a passion of secret woes,
She bore me under the rose.

One who my Mother nursed
Took me from the first: −
'O nurse, let me look upon
This babe that costs so dear;
Tomorrow she will be gone:
Other mothers may keep
Their babes awake and asleep,
But I must not keep her here.' −
Whether I know or guess,
I know this not the less.

So I was sent away
That none might spy the truth:
And my childhood waxed to youth
And I left off childish play.
I never cared to play
With the village boys and girls;
And I think they thought me proud,
I found so little to say
And kept so from the crowd:
But I had the longest curls,
And I had the largest eyes,
And my teeth were small like pearls;
The girls might flout and scout me,
But the boys would hang about me
In sheepish mooning wise.

Our one-street village stood
A long mile from the town,
A mile of windy down
And bleak one-sided wood,
With not a single house.
Our town itself was small,
With just the common shops,
And throve in its small way.
Our neighbouring gentry reared
The good old-fashioned crops,
And made old-fashioned boasts
Of what John Bull would do
If Frenchman Frog appeared,
And drank old-fashioned toasts,
And made old-fashioned bows
To my Lady at the Hall.

My Lady at the Hall
Is grander than they all:
Hers is the oldest name
In all the neighbourhood;
But the race must die with her
Tho' she's a lofty dame,
For she's unmarried still.
Poor people say she's good
And has an open hand
As any in the land,
And she's the comforter
Of many sick and sad;
My nurse once said to me
That everything she had
Came of my Lady's bounty:
'Tho' she's greatest in the county
She's humble to the poor,
No beggar seeks her door
But finds help presently.
I pray both night and day
For her, and you must pray:
But she'll never feel distress
If needy folk can bless.'

I was a little maid
When here we came to live
From somewhere by the sea.
Men spoke a foreign tongue
There where we used to be
When I was merry and young,
Too young to feel afraid;
The fisher-folk would give

A kind strange word to me,
There by the foreign sea:
I don't know where it was,
But I remember still
Our cottage on a hill,
And fields of flowering grass
On that fair foreign shore.

I liked my old home best,
But this was pleasant too:
So here we made our nest
And here I grew.
And now and then my Lady
In riding past our door
Would nod to Nurse and speak,
Or stoop and pat my cheek;
And I was always ready
To hold the field-gate wide
For my Lady to go thro';
My Lady in her veil
So seldom put aside,
My Lady grave and pale.

I often sat to wonder
Who might my parents be,
For I knew of something under
My simple-seeming state.
Nurse never talked to me
Of mother or of father,
But watched me early and late
With kind suspicious cares:
Or not suspicious, rather

Anxious, as if she knew
Some secret I might gather
And smart for unawares.
Thus I grew.

But Nurse waxed old and gray,
Bent and weak with years.
There came a certain day
That she lay upon her bed
Shaking her palsied head,
With words she gasped to say
Which had to stay unsaid.
Then with a jerking hand
Held out so piteously
She gave a ring to me
Of gold wrought curiously,
A ring which she had worn
Since the day that I was born,
She once had said to me:
I slipped it on my finger;
Her eyes were keen to linger
On my hand that slipped it on;
Then she sighed one rattling sigh
And stared on with sightless eye: —
The one who loved me was gone.

How long I stayed alone
With the corpse I never knew,
For I fainted dead as stone:
When I came to life once more
I was down upon the floor,
With neighbours making ado

To bring me back to life.
I heard the sexton's wife
Say: 'Up, my lad, and run
To tell it at the Hall;
She was my Lady's nurse,
And done can't be undone.
I'll watch by this poor lamb.
I guess my Lady's purse
Is always open to such:
I'd run up on my crutch
A cripple as I am,'
(For cramps had vexed her much,)
'Rather than this dear heart
Lack one to take her part.'

For days, day after day,
On my weary bed I lay,
Wishing the time would pass;
O, so wishing that I was
Likely to pass away:
For the one friend whom I knew
Was dead, I knew no other,
Neither father nor mother;
And I, what should I do?

One day the sexton's wife
Said: 'Rouse yourself, my dear:
My Lady has driven down
From the Hall into the town,
And we think she's coming here.
Cheer up, for life is life.'

But I would not look or speak,
Would not cheer up at all.
My tears were like to fall,
So I turned round to the wall
And hid my hollow cheek,
Making as if I slept,
As silent as a stone,
And no one knew I wept.
What was my Lady to me,
The grand lady from the Hall?
She might come, or stay away,
I was sick at heart that day:
The whole world seemed to be
Nothing, just nothing to me,
For aught that I could see.

Yet I listened where I lay:
A bustle came below,
A clear voice said: 'I know;
I will see her first alone,
It may be less of a shock
If she's so weak today:' –
A light hand turned the lock,
A light step crossed the floor,
One sat beside my bed:
But never a word she said.

For me, my shyness grew
Each moment more and more:
So I said never a word
And neither looked nor stirred;
I think she must have heard

My heart go pit-a-pat:
Thus I lay, my Lady sat,
More than a mortal hour
(I counted one and two
By the house-clock while I lay):
I seemed to have no power
To think of a thing to say,
Or do what I ought to do,
Or rouse myself to a choice.

At last she said: 'Margaret,
Won't you even look at me?'
A something in her voice
Forced my tears to fall at last,
Forced sobs from me thick and fast;
Something not of the past,
Yet stirring memory;
A something new, and yet
Not new, too sweet to last,
Which I never can forget.

I turned and stared at her:
Her cheek showed hollow-pale;
Her hair like mine was fair,
A wonderful fall of hair
That screened her like a veil;
But her height was statelier,
Her eyes had depth more deep:
I think they must have had
Always a something sad,
Unless they were asleep.

While I stared, my Lady took
My hand in her spare hand,
Jewelled and soft and grand,
And looked with a long long look
Of hunger in my face;
As if she tried to trace
Features she ought to know,
And half hoped, half feared, to find.
Whatever was in her mind
She heaved a sigh at last,
And began to talk to me.

'Your nurse was my dear nurse,
And her nursling's dear,' said she:
'No one told me a word
Of her getting worse and worse,
Till her poor life was past'
(Here my Lady's tears dropped fast):
'I might have been with her,
I might have promised and heard,
But she had no comforter.
She might have told me much
Which now I shall never know,
Never, never shall know.'
She sat by me sobbing so,
And seemed so woe-begone,
That I laid one hand upon
Hers with a timid touch,
Scarce thinking what I did,
Not knowing what to say:
That moment her face was hid
In the pillow close by mine,

Her arm was flung over me,
She hugged me, sobbing so
As if her heart would break,
And kissed me where I lay.

After this she often came
To bring me fruit or wine,
Or sometimes hothouse flowers.
And at nights I lay awake
Often and often thinking
What to do for her sake.
Wet or dry it was the same:
She would come in at all hours,
Set me eating and drinking,
And say I must grow strong;
At last the day seemed long
And home seemed scarcely home
If she did not come.

Well, I grew strong again:
In time of primroses
I went to pluck them in the lane;
In time of nestling birds
I heard them chirping round the house;
And all the herds
Were out at grass when I grew strong,
And days were waxen long,
And there was work for bees
Among the May-bush boughs,
And I had shot up tall,
And life felt after all

Pleasant, and not so long
When I grew strong.

I was going to the Hall
To be my Lady's maid:
'Her little friend,' she said to me,
'Almost her child,'
She said and smiled,
Sighing painfully;
Blushing, with a second flush,
As if she blushed to blush.

Friend, servant, child: just this
My standing at the Hall;
The other servants call me 'Miss,'
My Lady calls me 'Margaret,'
With her clear voice musical.
She never chides when I forget
This or that; she never chides.
Except when people come to stay
(And that's not often) at the Hall,
I sit with her all day
And ride out when she rides.
She sings to me and makes me sing;
Sometimes I read to her,
Sometimes we merely sit and talk.
She noticed once my ring
And made me tell its history:
That evening in our garden walk
She said she should infer
The ring had been my father's first,
Then my mother's, given for me

To the nurse who nursed
My mother in her misery,
That so quite certainly
Some one might know me, who ...
Then she was silent, and I too.

I hate when people come:
The women speak and stare
And mean to be so civil.
This one will stroke my hair,
That one will pat my cheek
And praise my Lady's kindness,
Expecting me to speak;
I like the proud ones best
Who sit as struck with blindness,
As if I wasn't there.
But if any gentleman
Is staying at the Hall
(Tho'few come prying here),
My Lady seems to fear
Some downright dreadful evil,
And makes me keep my room
As closely as she can:
So I hate when people come,
It is so troublesome.
In spite of all her care,
Sometimes to keep alive
I sometimes do contrive
To get out in the grounds
For a whiff of wholesome air,
Under the rose you know:
It's charming to break bounds,

Stolen waters are sweet,
And what's the good of feet
If for days they mustn't go?
Give me a longer tether,
Or I may break from it.

Now I have eyes and ears
And just some little wit:
'Almost my lady's child;'
I recollect she smiled,
Sighed and blushed together;
Then her story of the ring
Sounds not improbable,
She told it me so well
It seemed the actual thing: —
Oh, keep your counsel close,
But I guess under the rose,
In long past summer weather
When the world was blossoming,
And the rose upon its thorn:
I guess not who he was
Flawed honour like a glass
And made my life forlorn;
But my Mother, Mother, Mother,
Oh, I know her from all other.

My Lady, you might trust
Your daughter with your fame.
Trust me, I would not shame
Our honorable name,
For I have noble blood
Tho' I was bred in dust

And brought up in the mud.
I will not press my claim,
Just leave me where you will:
But you might trust your daughter,
For blood is thicker than water
And you're my mother still.

So my Lady holds her own
With condescending grace,
And fills her lofty place
With an untroubled face
As a queen may fill a throne.
While I could hint a tale –
(But then I am her child) –
Would make her quail;
Would set her in the dust,
Lorn with no comforter,
Her glorious hair defiled
And ashes on her cheek:
The decent world would thrust
Its finger out at her,
Not much displeased I think
To make a nine days' stir;
The decent world would sink
Its voice to speak of her.

Now this is what I mean
To do, no more, no less:
Never to speak, or show
Bare sign of what I know.
Let the blot pass unseen;
Yea, let her never guess

I hold the tangled clue
She huddles out of view.
Friend, servant, almost child,
So be it and nothing more
On this side of the grave.
Mother, in Paradise,
You'll see with clearer eyes;
Perhaps in this world even
When you are like to die
And face to face with Heaven
You'll drop for once the lie:
But you must drop the mask,
    not I.

My Lady promises
Two hundred pounds with me
Whenever I may wed
A man she can approve:
And since besides her bounty
I'm fairest in the county
(For so I've heard it said,
Tho' I don't vouch for this),
Her promised pounds may move
Some honest man to see
My virtues and my beauties;
Perhaps the rising grazier,
Or temperance publican,
May claim my wifely duties.
Meanwhile I wait their leisure
And grace-bestowing pleasure,
I wait the happy man;
But if I hold my head

And pitch my expectations
Just higher than their level,
They must fall back on patience:
I may not mean to wed,
Yet I'll be civil.

Now sometimes in a dream
My heart goes out of me
To build and scheme,
Till I sob after things that seem
So pleasant in a dream:
A home such as I see
My blessed neighbours live in
With father and with mother,
All proud of one another,
Named by one common name
From baby in the bud
To full-blown workman father;
It's little short of Heaven.
I'd give my gentle blood
To wash my special shame
And drown my private grudge;
I'd toil and moil much rather
The dingiest cottage drudge
Whose mother need not blush,
Than live here like a lady
And see my Mother flush
And hear her voice unsteady
Sometimes, yet never dare
Ask to share her care.

Of course the servants sneer
Behind my back at me;
Of course the village girls,
Who envy me my curls
And gowns and idleness,
Take comfort in a jeer;
Of course the ladies guess
Just so much of my history
As points the emphatic stress
With which they laud my Lady;
The gentlemen who catch
A casual glimpse of me
And turn again to see,
Their valets on the watch
To speak a word with me,
All know and sting me wild;
Till I am almost ready
To wish that I were dead,
No faces more to see,
No more words to be said,
My Mother safe at last
Disburdened of her child,
And the past past.

'All equal before God,' –
Our Rector has it so,
And sundry sleepers nod:
It may be so; I know
All are not equal here,
And when the sleepers wake
They make a difference.
'All equal in the grave,' –

That shows an obvious sense:
Yet something which I crave
Not death itself brings near;
How should death half atone
For all my past; or make
The name I bear my own?

I love my dear old Nurse
Who loved me without gains;
I love my mistress even,
Friend, Mother, what you will:
But I could almost curse
My Father for his pains;
And sometimes at my prayer,
Kneeling in sight of Heaven,
I almost curse him still:
Why did he set his snare
To catch at unaware
My Mother's foolish youth;
Load me with shame that's hers,
And her with something worse,
A lifelong lie for truth?

I think my mind is fixed
On one point and made up:
To accept my lot unmixed;
Never to drug the cup
But drink it by myself.
I'll not be wooed for pelf;
I'll not blot out my shame
With any man's good name;
But nameless as I stand,

My hand is my own hand,
And nameless as I came
I go to the dark land.

'All equal in the grave,' –
I bide my time till then:
'All equal before God,' –
Today I feel His rod,
Tomorrow He may save:
   Amen.

Resurgam

From depth to height, from height to loftier height,
　　The climber sets his foot and sets his face,
　　Tracks lingering sunbeams to their halting-place,
And counts the last pulsations of the light.
Strenuous thro' day and unsurprised by night
　　He runs a race with Time, and wins the race,
　　Emptied and stripped of all save only Grace,
Will, Love, a threefold panoply of might.
Darkness descends for light he toiled to seek:
　　He stumbles on the darkened mountain-head,
　　Left breathless in the unbreathable thin air,
　　Made freeman of the living and the dead: –
He wots not he has topped the topmost peak,
　　But the returning sun will find him there.

My Dream

Hear now a curious dream I dreamed last night,
Each word whereof is weighed and sifted truth.

I stood beside Euphrates while it swelled
Like overflowing Jordan in its youth:
It waxed and coloured sensibly to sight,
Till out of myriad pregnant waves there welled
Young crocodiles, a gaunt blunt-featured crew,
Fresh-hatched perhaps and daubed with birthday dew.
The rest if I should tell, I fear my friend,
My closest friend, would deem the facts untrue;
And therefore it were wisely left untold;
Yet if you will, why, hear it to the end.

Each crocodile was girt with massive gold
And polished stones, that with their wearers grew:
But one there was who waxed beyond the rest,
Wore kinglier girdle and a kingly crown,
Whilst crowns and orbs and sceptres starred his breast.
All gleamed compact and green with scale on scale,
But special burnishment adorned his mail,
And special terror weighed upon his frown;
His punier brethren quaked before his tail,
Broad as a rafter, potent as a flail.
So he grew lord and master of his kin:
But who shall tell the tale of all their woes?
An execrable appetite arose,
He battened on them, crunched, and sucked them in.
He knew no law, he feared no binding law,
But ground them with inexorable jaw:

The luscious fat distilled upon his chin,
Exuded from his nostrils and his eyes,
While still like hungry death he fed his maw;
Till every minor crocodile being dead
And buried too, himself gorged to the full,
He slept with breath oppressed and unstrung claw.
Oh marvel passing strange which next I saw:
In sleep he dwindled to the common size,
And all the empire faded from his coat.
Then from far off a wingèd vessel came,
Swift as a swallow, subtle as a flame:
I know not what it bore of freight or host,
But white it was as an avenging ghost.
It levelled strong Euphrates in its course;
Supreme yet weightless as an idle mote
It seemed to tame the waters without force
Till not a murmur swelled or billow beat:
Lo, as the purple shadow swept the sands,
The prudent crocodile rose on his feet
And shed appropriate tears and wrung his hands.

What can it mean? you ask. I answer not
For meaning, but myself must echo, What?
And tell it as I saw it on the spot.

An End

Love, strong as Death, is dead.
Come, let us make his bed
Among the dying flowers:
A green turf at his head;
And a stone at his feet,
Whereon we may sit
In the quiet evening hours.

He was born in the Spring,
And died before the harvesting:
On the last warm Summer day
He left us; he would not stay
For Autumn twilight cold and gray.
Sit we by his grave, and sing
He is gone away.

To few chords and sad and low
Sing we so:
Be our eyes fixed on the grass
Shadow-veiled as the years pass,
While we think of all that was
In the long ago.

Sweet Death

The sweetest blossoms die.
    And so it was that, going day by day
    Unto the church to praise and pray,
And crossing the green churchyard thoughtfully,
    I saw how on the graves the flowers
    Shed their fresh leaves in showers,
And how their perfume rose up to the sky
    Before it passed away.

The youngest blossoms die.
    They die and fall and nourish the rich earth
    From which they lately had their birth;
Sweet life, but sweeter death that passeth by
    And is as though it had not been: —
    All colours turn to green;
The bright hues vanish and the odours fly,
    The grass hath lasting worth.

And youth and beauty die.
    So be it, O my God, Thou God of truth:
    Better than beauty and than youth
Are Saints and Angels, a glad company;
    And Thou, O Lord, our Rest and Ease,
    Art better far than these.
Why should we shrink from our full harvest? why
    Prefer to glean with Ruth?

Dream-Love

Young Love lies sleeping
    In May-time of the year,
Among the lilies,
    Lapped in the tender light:
White lambs come grazing,
    White doves come building there;
And round about him
    The May-bushes are white.

Soft moss the pillow
    For Oh, a softer cheek;
Broad leaves cast shadow
    Upon the heavy eyes:
There winds and waters
    Grow lulled and scarcely speak;
There twilight lingers
    The longest in the skies.

Young Love lies dreaming;
    But who shall tell the dream?
A perfect sunlight
    On rustling forest tips;
Or perfect moonlight
    Upon a rippling stream;
Or perfect silence,
    Or song of cherished lips.

Burn odours round him
    To fill the drowsy air;
Weave silent dances

Around him to and fro;
For Oh, in waking,
    The sights are not so fair,
And song and silence
    Are not like these below.

Young Love lies dreaming
    Till summer days are gone,
Dreaming and drowsing
    Away to perfect sleep:
He sees the beauty
    Sun hath not looked upon,
And tastes the fountain
    Unutterably deep.

Him perfect music
    Doth hush unto his rest,
And thro' the pauses
    The perfect silence calms:
Oh, poor the voices
    Of earth from east to west,
And poor earth's stillness
    Between her stately palms.

Young Love lies drowsing
    Away to poppied death;
Cool shadows deepen
    Across the sleeping face:
So fails the summer
    With warm, delicious breath;
And what hath autumn
    To give us in its place?

Draw close the curtains
        Of branched evergreen;
Change cannot touch them
        With fading fingers sere:
Here the first violets
        Perhaps will bud unseen,
And a dove, may be,
        Return to nestle here.

Symbols

I watched a rosebud very long
    Brought on by dew and sun and shower,
    Waiting to see the perfect flower:
Then, when I thought it should be strong,
    It opened at the matin hour
And fell at evensong.

I watched a nest from day to day,
    A green nest full of pleasant shade,
    Wherein three speckled eggs were laid:
But when they should have hatched in May,
    The two old birds had grown afraid
Or tired, and flew away.

Then in my wrath I broke the bough
    That I had tended so with care,
    Hoping its scent should fill the air;
I crushed the eggs, not heeding how
    Their ancient promise had been fair:
I would have vengeance now.

But the dead branch spoke from the sod,
    And the eggs answered me again:
    Because we failed dost thou complain?
Is thy wrath just? And what if God,
    Who waiteth for thy fruits in vain,
Should also take the rod?

One Sea-Side Grave

Unmindful of the roses,
    Unmindful of the thorn,
A reaper tired reposes
    Among his gathered corn:
    So might I, till the morn!

Cold as the cold Decembers,
    Past as the days that set,
While only one remembers
    And all the rest forget, —
    But one remembers yet.

Martyrs' Song

We meet in joy, tho'we part in sorrow;
We part tonight, but we meet tomorrow.
Be it flood or blood the path that's trod,
All the same it leads home to God:
Be it furnace-fire voluminous,
One like God's Son will walk with us.

What are these that glow from afar,
These that lean over the golden bar,
Strong as the lion, pure as the dove,
With open arms and hearts of love?
They the blessed ones gone before,
They the blessed for evermore.
Out of great tribulation they went
Home to their home of Heaven-content;
Thro' flood, or blood, or furnace-fire,
To the rest that fulfils desire.

What are these that fly as a cloud,
With flashing heads and faces bowed,
In their mouths a victorious psalm,
In their hands a robe and a palm?
Welcoming angels these that shine,
Your own angel, and yours, and mine;
Who have hedged us both day and night
On the left hand and on the right,
Who have watched us both night and day
Because the Devil keeps watch to slay.

Light above light, and Bliss beyond bliss,
Whom words cannot utter, lo, Who is This?
As a King with many crowns He stands,
And our names are graven upon His hands;
As a Priest, with God-uplifted eyes,
He offers for us His Sacrifice;
As the Lamb of God for sinners slain,
That we too may live He lives again;
As our Champion behold Him stand,
Strong to save us, at God's Right Hand.

God the Father give us grace
To walk in the light of Jesus' Face.
God the Son give us a part
In the hiding-place of Jesus' Heart:
God the Spirit so hold us up
That we may drink of Jesus' cup.

Death is short and life is long;
Satan is strong, but Christ more strong.
At His Word, Who hath led us hither,
The Red Sea must part hither and thither.
At His Word, Who goes before us too,
Jordan must cleave to let us thro'.

Yet one pang, searching and sore,
And then Heaven forevermore;
Yet one moment awful and dark,
Then safety within the Veil and the Ark;
Yet one effort by Christ His grace,
Then Christ forever face to face.

God the Father we will adore,
In Jesus' Name, now and evermore:
God the Son we will love and thank
In this flood and on the farther bank:
God the Holy Ghost we will praise,
In Jesus' Name, thro' endless days:
God Almighty, God Three in One,
God Almighty, God alone.

A Wintry Sonnet

A Robin said: The Spring will never come,
    And I shall never care to build again.
A Rosebush said: These frosts are wearisome,
    My sap will never stir for sun or rain.
The half Moon said: These nights are fogged and slow,
    I neither care to wax nor care to wane.
The Ocean said: I thirst from long ago,
    Because earth's rivers cannot fill the main. –
When Springtime came, red Robin built a nest,
    And trilled a lover's song in sheer delight.
    Gray hoarfrost vanished, and the Rose with might
    Clothed her in leaves and buds of crimson core.
The dim Moon brightened. Ocean sunned his crest,
    Dimpled his blue, – yet thirsted evermore.

The Hour and the Ghost

BRIDE
O love, love, hold me fast, –
He draws me away from thee;
I cannot stem the blast,
Nor the cold strong sea:
Far away a light shines
Beyond the hills and pines;
It is lit for me.

BRIDEGROOM
I have thee close, my dear,
No terror can come near;
Only far off the northern light shines clear.

GHOST
Come with me, fair and false,
To our home, come home.
It is my voice that calls:
Once thou wast not afraid
When I wooed, and said,
'Come, our nest is newly made,' –
Now cross the tossing foam.

BRIDE
Hold me one moment longer,
He taunts me with the past,
His clutch is waxing stronger,
Hold me fast, hold me fast.
He draws me from thy heart,
And I cannot withhold:

He bids my spirit depart
With him into the cold: —
O bitter vows of old!

BRIDEGROOM
Lean on me, hide thine eyes:
Only ourselves, earth and skies,
Are present here: be wise.

GHOST
Lean on me, come away,
I will guide and steady:
Come, for I will not stay:
Come, for house and bed are ready.
Ah, sure bed and house,
For better and worse, for life and death:
Goal won with shortened breath:
Come, crown our vows.

BRIDE
One moment, one more word,
While my heart beats still,
While my breath is stirred
By my fainting will.
O friend forsake me not,
Forget not as I forgot:
But keep thy heart for me,
Keep thy faith true and bright;
Thro' the lone cold winter night
Perhaps I may come to thee.

BRIDEGROOM
Nay, peace, my darling, peace:
Let these dreams and terrors cease:
Who spoke of death or change or aught but ease?

GHOST
O fair frail sin,
O poor harvest gathered in!
Thou shalt visit him again
To watch his heart grow cold;
To know the gnawing pain
I knew of old;
To see one much more fair
Fill up the vacant chair,
Fill his heart, his children bear: —
While thou and I together
In the outcast weather
Toss and howl and spin.

Today's Burden

'Arise, depart, for this is not your rest.' –
  Oh, burden of all burdens, still to arise
  And still depart, nor rest in any wise!
Rolling, still rolling thus to east from west,
Earth journeys on her immemorial quest,
  Whom a moon chases in no different guise:
  Thus stars pursue their courses, and thus flies
The sun, and thus all creatures manifest
Unrest the common heritage, the ban
  Flung broadcast on all humankind, on all
   Who live; for living, all are bound to die:
That which is old, we know that it is man:
   These have no rest who sit and dream and sigh,
   Nor have those rest who wrestle and who fall.

An Apple Gathering

I plucked pink blossoms from mine apple tree,
    And wore them all that evening in my hair:
Then in due season when I went to see
    I found no apples there.

With dangling basket all along the grass
    As I had come I went the selfsame track:
My neighbours mocked me while they saw me pass
    So empty-handed back.

Lilian and Lilias smiled in trudging by,
    Their heaped-up basket teased me like a jeer;
Sweet-voiced they sang beneath the sunset sky,
    Their mother's home was near.

Plump Gertrude passed me with her basket full,
    A stronger hand than hers helped it along;
A voice talked with her thro' the shadows cool
    More sweet to me than song.

Ah, Willie, Willie, was my love less worth
    Than apples with their green leaves piled above?
I counted rosiest apples on the earth
    Of far less worth than love.

So once it was with me you stooped to talk
    Laughing and listening in this very lane:
To think that by this way we used to walk
    We shall not walk again!

I let my neighbours pass me, ones and twos
    And groups; the latest said the night grew chill,
And hastened: but I loitered, while the dews
    Fell fast I loitered still.

A Summer Wish

Live all thy sweet life thro',
    Sweet Rose, dew-sprent,
Drop down thine evening dew
To gather it anew
When day is bright:
    I fancy thou wast meant
Chiefly to give delight.

Sing in the silent sky,
    Glad soaring bird;
Sing out thy notes on high
To sunbeam straying by
Or passing cloud;
    Heedless if thou art heard
Sing thy full song aloud.

Oh that it were with me
    As with the flower;
Blooming on its own tree
For butterfly and bee
Its summer morns:
    That I might bloom mine hour
A rose in spite of thorns.

Oh that my work were done
    As birds' that soar
Rejoicing in the sun:
That when my time is run
And daylight too,
    I so might rest once more
Cool with refreshing dew.

Up-Hill

Does the road wind up-hill all the way?
    Yes, to the very end.
Will the day's journey take the whole long day?
    From morn to night, my friend.

But is there for the night a resting-place?
    A roof for when the slow dark hours begin.
May not the darkness hide it from my face?
    You cannot miss that inn.

Shall I meet other wayfarers at night?
    Those who have gone before.
Then must I knock, or call when just in sight?
    They will not keep you standing at that door.

Shall I find comfort, travel-sore and weak?
    Of labour you shall find the sum.
Will there be beds for me and all who seek?
    Yea, beds for all who come.

Bitter for Sweet

Summer is gone with all its roses,
    Its sun and perfumes and sweet flowers,
    Its warm air and refreshing showers:
        And even Autumn closes.

Yea, Autumn's chilly self is going,
    And winter comes which is yet colder;
    Each day the hoar-frost waxes bolder,
        And the last buds cease blowing.

The Convent Threshold

There's blood between us, love, my love,
There's father's blood, there's brother's blood;
And blood's a bar I cannot pass:
I choose the stairs that mount above,
Stair after golden skyward stair,
To city and to sea of glass.
My lily feet are soiled with mud,
With scarlet mud which tells a tale
Of hope that was, of guilt that was,
Of love that shall not yet avail;
Alas, my heart, if I could bare
My heart, this selfsame stain is there:
I seek the sea of glass and fire
To wash the spot, to burn the snare;
Lo, stairs are meant to lift us higher:
Mount with me, mount the kindled stair.

Your eyes look earthward, mine look up.
I see the far-off city grand,
Beyond the hills a watered land,
Beyond the gulf a gleaming strand
Of mansions where the righteous sup;
Who sleep at ease among their trees,
Or wake to sing a cadenced hymn
With Cherubim and Seraphim;
They bore the Cross, they drained the cup,
Racked, roasted, crushed, wrenched limb from limb,
They the offscouring of the world:
The heaven of starry heavens unfurled,
The sun before their face is dim.

You looking earthward, what see you?
Milk-white, wine-flushed among the vines,
Up and down leaping, to and fro,
Most glad, most full, made strong with wines,
Blooming as peaches pearled with dew,
Their golden windy hair afloat,
Love-music warbling in their throat,
Young men and women come and go.

You linger, yet the time is short:
Flee for your life, gird up your strength
To flee; the shadows stretched at length
Show that day wanes, that night draws nigh;
Flee to the mountain, tarry not.
Is this a time for smile and sigh,
For songs among the secret trees
Where sudden blue birds nest and sport?
The time is short and yet you stay:
Today, while it is called today,
Kneel, wrestle, knock, do violence, pray;
Today is short, tomorrow nigh:
Why will you die? why will you die?

You sinned with me a pleasant sin:
Repent with me, for I repent.
Woe's me the lore I must unlearn!
Woe's me that easy way we went,
So rugged when I would return!
How long until my sleep begin,
How long shall stretch these nights and days?
Surely, clean Angels cry, she prays;

She laves her soul with tedious tears:
How long must stretch these years and years?

I turn from you my cheeks and eyes,
My hair which you shall see no more, –
Alas for joy that went before,
For joy that dies, for love that dies.
Only my lips still turn to you,
My livid lips that cry, Repent!
Oh weary life, Oh weary Lent,
Oh weary time whose stars are few!

How should I rest in Paradise,
Or sit on steps of Heaven alone?
If Saints and Angels spoke of love
Should I not answer from my throne?
Have pity upon me, ye my friends,
For I have heard the sound thereof:
Should I not turn with yearning eyes,
Turn earthwards with a pitiful pang?
Oh save me from a pang in Heaven!
By all the gifts we took and gave,
Repent, repent, and be forgiven:
This life is long, but yet it ends;
Repent and purge your soul and save:
No gladder song the morning stars
Upon their birthday morning sang
Than Angels sing when one repents.

I tell you what I dreamed last night:
A spirit with transfigured face
Fire-footed clomb an infinite space.

I heard his hundred pinions clang,
Heaven-bells rejoicing rang and rang,
Heaven-air was thrilled with subtle scents,
Worlds spun upon their rushing cars:
He mounted shrieking: 'Give me light!'
Still light was poured on him, more light;
Angels, Archangels he outstripped,
Exultant in exceeding might,
And trod the skirts of Cherubim.
Still 'Give me light,' he shrieked; and dipped
His thirsty face, and drank a sea,
Athirst with thirst it could not slake.
I saw him, drunk with knowledge, take
From aching brows the aureole crown —
His locks writhed like a cloven snake —
He left his throne to grovel down
And lick the dust of Seraphs' feet:
For what is knowledge duly weighed?
Knowledge is strong, but love is sweet;
Yea, all the progress he had made
Was but to learn that all is small
Save love, for love is all in all.

I tell you what I dreamed last night:
It was not dark, it was not light,
Cold dews had drenched my plenteous hair
Thro' clay; you came to seek me there.
And 'Do you dream of me?' you said.
My heart was dust that used to leap
To you; I answered half asleep:
'My pillow is damp, my sheets are red,
There's a leaden tester to my bed:

Find you a warmer playfellow,
A warmer pillow for your head,
A kinder love to love than mine.'
You wrung your hands; while I like lead
Crushed downwards thro' the sodden earth:
You smote your hands but not in mirth,
And reeled but were not drunk with wine.

For all night long I dreamed of you:
I woke and prayed against my will,
Then slept to dream of you again.
At length I rose and knelt and prayed:
I cannot write the words I said,
My words were slow, my tears were few;
But thro' the dark my silence spoke
Like thunder. When this morning broke,
My face was pinched, my hair was grey,
And frozen blood was on the sill
Where stifling in my struggle I lay.

If now you saw me you would say:
Where is the face I used to love?
And I would answer: Gone before;
It tarries veiled in Paradise.
When once the morning star shall rise,
When earth with shadow flees away
And we stand safe within the door,
Then you shall lift the veil thereof.
Look up, rise up: for far above
Our palms are grown, our place is set;
There we shall meet as once we met,
And love with old familiar love.

Rest

O Earth, lie heavily upon her eyes;
    Seal her sweet eyes weary of watching, Earth;
    Lie close around her; leave no room for mirth
With its harsh laughter, nor for sound of sighs.
She hath no questions, she hath no replies,
    Hushed in and curtained with a blessèd dearth
    Of all that irked her from the hour of birth;
With stillness that is almost Paradise.
Darkness more clear than noon-day holdeth her,
    Silence more musical than any song;
Even her very heart has ceased to stir:
Until the morning of Eternity
Her rest shall not begin nor end, but be;
    And when she wakes she will not think it long.

Dead Before Death

Ah! changed and cold, how changed and very cold!
    With stiffened smiling lips and cold calm eyes:
    Changed, yet the same; much knowing, little wise;
This was the promise of the days of old!
Grown hard and stubborn in the ancient mould,
    Grown rigid in the sham of lifelong lies:
    We hoped for better things as years would rise,
But it is over as a tale once told.
All fallen the blossom that no fruitage bore,
    All lost the present and the future time,
All lost, all lost, the lapse that went before:
So lost till death shut-to the opened door,
    So lost from chime to everlasting chime,
So cold and lost for ever evermore.

Noble Sisters

'Now did you mark a falcon,
    Sister dear, sister dear,
Flying toward my window
    In the morning cool and clear?
With jingling bells about her neck,
    But what beneath her wing?
It may have been a ribbon,
    Or it may have been a ring.' –
    'I marked a falcon swooping
      At the break of day:
    And for your love, my sister dove,
      I 'frayed the thief away.' –

'Or did you spy a ruddy hound,
    Sister fair and tall,
Went snuffing round my garden bound,
    Or crouched by my bower wall?
With a silken leash about his neck;
    But in his mouth may be
A chain of gold and silver links,
    Or a letter writ to me.' –
    'I heard a hound, highborn sister,
      Stood baying at the moon:
    I rose and drove him from your wall
      Lest you should wake too soon.' –

'Or did you meet a pretty page
    Sat swinging on the gate;

Sat whistling, whistling like a bird,
    Or may be slept too late:
With eaglets broidered on his cap,
    And eaglets on his glove?
If you had turned his pockets out,
    You had found some pledge of love.' –
      'I met him at this daybreak,
        Scarce the east was red:
      Lest the creaking gate should anger you,
        I packed him home to bed.' –

'Oh patience, sister. Did you see
    A young man tall and strong,
Swift-footed to uphold the right
    And to uproot the wrong,
Come home across the desolate sea
    To woo me for his wife?
And in his heart my heart is locked,
    And in his life my life.' –
      'I met a nameless man, sister,
        Who loitered round our door:
      I said: Her husband loves her much.
        And yet she loves him more.' –

'Fie, sister, fie, a wicked lie,
    A lie, a wicked lie;
I have none other love but him,
    Nor will have till I die.
And you have turned him from our door,
    And stabbed him with a lie:

I will go seek him thro' the world
　　In sorrow till I die.' –
　　　'Go seek in sorrow, sister,
　　　　And find in sorrow too:
　　　If thus you shame our father's name
　　　　My curse go forth with you.'

From House to Home

The first was like a dream thro' summer heat,
    The second like a tedious numbing swoon,
While the half-frozen pulses lagged to beat
    Beneath a winter moon.

'But,' says my friend, 'what was this thing and where?'
    It was a pleasure-place within my soul;
An earthly paradise supremely fair
    That lured me from the goal.

The first part was a tissue of hugged lies;
    The second was its ruin fraught with pain:
Why raise the fair delusion to the skies
    But to be dashed again?

My castle stood of white transparent glass
    Glittering and frail with many a fretted spire,
But when the summer sunset came to pass
    It kindled into fire.

My pleasaunce was an undulating green,
    Stately with trees whose shadows slept below,
With glimpses of smooth garden-beds between,
    Like flame or sky or snow.

Swift squirrels on the pastures took their ease,
    With leaping lambs safe from the unfeared knife;
All singing-birds rejoicing in those trees
    Fulfilled their careless life.

Wood-pigeons cooed there, stock-doves nestled there;
　　My trees were full of songs and flowers and fruit,
Their branches spread a city to the air,
　　And mice lodged in their root.

My heath lay farther off, where lizards lived
　　In strange metallic mail, just spied and gone;
Like darted lightnings here and there perceived
　　But nowhere dwelt upon.

Frogs and fat toads were there to hop or plod
　　And propagate in peace, an uncouth crew,
Where velvet-headed rushes rustling nod
　　And spill the morning dew.

All caterpillars throve beneath my rule,
　　With snails and slugs in corners out of sight;
I never marred the curious sudden stool
　　That perfects in a night.

Safe in his excavated gallery
　　The burrowing mole groped on from year to year;
No harmless hedgehog curled because of me
　　His prickly back for fear.

Ofttimes one like an angel walked with me,
　　With spirit-discerning eyes like flames of fire,
But deep as the unfathomed endless sea
　　Fulfilling my desire:

And sometimes like a snowdrift he was fair,
　　And sometimes like a sunset glorious red,

And sometimes he had wings to scale the air
     With aureole round his head.

We sang our songs together by the way,
     Calls and recalls and echoes of delight;
So communed we together all the day,
     And so in dreams by night.

I have no words to tell what way we walked,
     What unforgotten path now closed and sealed;
I have no words to tell all things we talked,
     All things that he revealed:

This only can I tell: that hour by hour
     I waxed more feastful, lifted up and glad;
I felt no thorn-prick when I plucked a flower,
     Felt not my friend was sad.

'Tomorrow,' once I said to him with smiles:
     'Tonight,' he answered gravely and was dumb,
But pointed out the stones that numbered miles
     And miles and miles to come.

'Not so,' I said: 'tomorrow shall be sweet;
     Tonight is not so sweet as coming days.'
Then first I saw that he had turned his feet,
     Had turned from me his face:

Running and flying miles and miles he went,
     But once looked back to beckon with his hand
And cry: 'Come home, O love, from banishment:
     Come to the distant land.' –

That night destroyed me like an avalanche;
      One night turned all my summer back to snow:
Next morning not a bird upon my branch,
      Not a lamb woke below;

No bird, no lamb, no living breathing thing;
      No squirrel scampered on my breezy lawn,
No mouse lodged by his hoard: all joys took wing
      And fled before that dawn.

Azure and sun were starved from heaven above,
      No dew had fallen, but biting frost lay hoar:
O love, I knew that I should meet my love,
      Should find my love no more.

'My love no more,' I muttered, stunned with pain:
      I shed no tear, I wrung no passionate hand,
Till something whispered: 'You shall meet again,
      Meet in a distant land.'

Then with a cry like famine I arose,
      I lit my candle, searched from room to room,
Searched up and down; a war of winds that froze
      Swept thro' the blank of gloom.

I searched day after day, night after night;
      Scant change there came to me of night or day:
'No more,' I wailed, 'no more;' and trimmed my light,
      And gnashed, but did not pray,

Until my heart broke and my spirit broke:
      Upon the frost-bound floor I stumbled, fell,

And moaned: 'It is enough: withhold the stroke.
   Farewell, O love, farewell.'

Then life swooned from me. And I heard the song
   Of spheres and spirits rejoicing over me:
One cried: 'Our sister, she hath suffered long.' –
   One answered: 'Make her see.' –

One cried: 'Oh blessed she who no more pain,
   Who no more disappointment shall receive.' –
One answered: 'Not so: she must live again;
   Strengthen thou her to live.'

So while I lay entranced, a curtain seemed
   To shrivel with crackling from before my face,
Across mine eyes a waxing radiance beamed
   And showed a certain place.

I saw a vision of a woman, where
   Night and new morning strive for domination;
Incomparably pale, and almost fair,
   And sad beyond expression.

Her eyes were like some fire-enshrining gem,
   Were stately like the stars, and yet were tender;
Her figure charmed me like a windy stem
   Quivering and drooped and slender.

I stood upon the outer barren ground,
   She stood on inner ground that budded flowers;
While circling in their never-slackening round
   Danced by the mystic hours.

But every flower was lifted on a thorn,
    And every thorn shot upright from its sands
To gall her feet; hoarse laughter pealed in scorn
    With cruel clapping hands.

She bled and wept, yet did not shrink; her strength
    Was strung up until daybreak of delight:
She measured measureless sorrow toward its length,
    And breadth, and depth, and height.

Then marked I how a chain sustained her form,
    A chain of living links not made nor riven:
It stretched sheer up thro' lightning, wind, and storm,
    And anchored fast in heaven.

One cried: 'How long? yet founded on the Rock
    She shall do battle, suffer, and attain.' –
One answered: 'Faith quakes in the tempest shock:
    Strengthen her soul again.'

I saw a cup sent down and come to her
    Brimful of loathing and of bitterness:
She drank with livid lips that seemed to stir
    The depth, not make it less.

But as she drank I spied a hand distil
    New wine and virgin honey; making it
First bitter-sweet, then sweet indeed, until
    She tasted only sweet.

Her lips and cheeks waxed rosy-fresh and young;
    Drinking she sang: 'My soul shall nothing want;'

And drank anew: while soft a song was sung,
    A mystical slow chant.

One cried: 'The wounds are faithful of a friend:
    The wilderness shall blossom as a rose.' –
One answered: 'Rend the veil, declare the end,
    Strengthen her ere she goes.'

Then earth and heaven were rolled up like a scroll;
    Time and space, change and death, had passed away;
Weight, number, measure, each had reached its whole:
    The day had come, that day.

Multitudes – multitudes – stood up in bliss,
    Made equal to the angels, glorious, fair;
With harps, palms, wedding-garments, kiss of peace,
    And crowned and haloed hair.

They sang a song, a new song in the height,
    Harping with harps to Him Who is Strong and True:
They drank new wine, their eyes saw with new light,
    Lo, all things were made new.

Tier beyond tier they rose and rose and rose
    So high that it was dreadful, flames with flames:
No man could number them, no tongue disclose
    Their secret sacred names.

As tho' one pulse stirred all, one rush of blood
    Fed all, one breath swept thro' them myriad-voiced,
They struck their harps, cast down their crowns, they stood
    And worshipped and rejoiced.

Each face looked one way like a moon new-lit,
    Each face looked one way towards its Sun of Love;
Drank love and bathed in love and mirrored it
    And knew no end thereof.

Glory touched glory on each blessed head,
    Hands locked dear hands never to sunder more:
These were the new-begotten from the dead
    Whom the great birthday bore.

Heart answered heart, soul answered soul at rest,
    Double against each other, filled, sufficed:
All loving, loved of all; but loving best
    And best beloved of Christ.

I saw that one who lost her love in pain,
    Who trod on thorns, who drank the loathsome cup;
The lost in night, in day was found again;
    The fallen was lifted up.

They stood together in the blessed noon,
    They sang together thro' the length of days;
Each loving face bent Sunwards like a moon
    New-lit with love and praise.

Therefore, O friend, I would not if I might
    Rebuild my house of lies, wherein I joyed
One time to dwell: my soul shall walk in white,
    Cast down but not destroyed.

Therefore in patience I possess my soul;
    Yea, therefore as a flint I set my face,

To pluck down, to build up again the whole –
     But in a distant place.

These thorns are sharp, yet I can tread on them;
     This cup is loathsome, yet He makes it sweet:
My face is steadfast toward Jerusalem,
     My heart remembers it.

I lift the hanging hands, the feeble knees –
     I, precious more than seven times molten gold –
Until the day when from His storehouses
     God shall bring new and old;

Beauty for ashes, oil of joy for grief,
     Garment of praise for spirit of heaviness:
Altho' today I fade as doth a leaf,
     I languish and grow less.

Altho' today He prunes my twigs with pain,
     Yet doth His blood nourish and warm my root:
Tomorrow I shall put forth buds again,
     And clothe myself with fruit.

Altho' today I walk in tedious ways,
     Today His staff is turned into a rod,
Yet will I wait for Him the appointed days
     And stay upon my God.

Bird Raptures

The sunrise wakes the lark to sing,
    The moonrise wakes the nightingale.
Come darkness, moonrise, everything
    That is so silent, sweet, and pale:
    Come, so ye wake the nightingale.

Make haste to mount, thou wistful moon,
    Make haste to wake the nightingale:
Let silence set the world in tune
    To hearken to that wordless tale
    Which warbles from the nightingale

O herald skylark, stay thy flight
    One moment, for a nightingale
Floods us with sorrow and delight.
    Tomorrow thou shalt hoist the sail;
Leave us tonight the nightingale.

Sleep at Sea

Sound the deep waters: —
    Who shall sound that deep? —
Too short the plummet,
    And the watchmen sleep.
Some dream of effort
    Up a toilsome steep;
Some dream of pasture grounds
    For harmless sheep.

White shapes flit to and fro
    From mast to mast;
They feel the distant tempest
    That nears them fast:
Great rocks are straight ahead,
    Great shoals not past;
They shout to one another
    Upon the blast.

Oh soft the streams drop music
    Between the hills,
And musical the birds' nests
    Beside those rills:
The nests are types of home
    Love-hidden from ills,
The nests are types of spirits
    Love-music fills.

So dream the sleepers,
    Each man in his place;
The lightning shows the smile

Upon each face:
The ship is driving, driving,
 It drives apace:
And sleepers smile, and spirits
 Bewail their case.

The lightning glares and reddens
 Across the skies;
It seems but sunset
 To those sleeping eyes.
When did the sun go down
 On such a wise?
From such a sunset
 When shall day arise?

'Wake,' call the spirits:
 But to heedless ears;
They have forgotten sorrows
 And hopes and fears;
They have forgotten perils
 And smiles and tears;
Their dream has held them long,
 Long years and years.

'Wake,' call the spirits again:
 But it would take
A louder summons
 To bid them awake.
Some dream of pleasure
 For another's sake;
Some dream, forgetful
 Of a lifelong ache.

One by one slowly,
    Ah, how sad and slow —
Wailing and praying
    The spirits rise and go:
Clear stainless spirits,
    White, as white as snow;
Pale spirits, wailing
    For an overthrow.

One by one flitting,
    Like a mournful bird
Whose song is tired at last
    For no mate heard.
The loving voice is silent,
    The useless word;
One by one flitting,
    Sick with hope deferred.

Driving and driving,
    The ship drives amain:
While swift from mast to mast
    Shapes flit again,
Flit silent as the silence
    Where men lie slain;
Their shadow cast upon the sails
    Is like a stain.

No voice to call the sleepers,
    No hand to raise:
They sleep to death in dreaming
    Of length of days.
Vanity of vanities,

The Preacher says:
Vanity is the end
Of all their ways.

My Friend

Two days ago with dancing glancing hair,
 With living lips and eyes:
 Now pale, dumb, blind, she lies;
So pale, yet still so fair.

We have not left her yet, not yet alone;
 But soon must leave her where
 She will not miss our care,
Bone of our bone.

Weep not; O friends, we should not weep:
 Our friend of friends lies full of rest;
 No sorrow rankles in her breast,
Fallen fast asleep.

She sleeps below,
 She wakes and laughs above;
 Today, as she walked, let us walk in love,
Tomorrow follow so.

Dead Hope

Hope new born one pleasant morn
    Died at even;
Hope dead lives nevermore,
    No, not in heaven.

If his shroud were but a cloud
    To weep itself away;
Or were he buried underground
    To sprout some day!
But dead and gone is dead and gone
    Vainly wept upon.

Nought we place above his face
    To mark the spot,
But it shows a barren place
    In our lot.
Hope has birth no more on earth
    Morn or even;
Hope dead lives nevermore,
    No, not in heaven.

Twilight Calm

O pleasant eventide!
Clouds on the western side
Grow grey and greyer, hiding the warm sun:
The bees and birds, their happy labors done,
Seek their close nests and bide.

Screened in the leafy wood
The stock-doves sit and brood:
The very squirrel leaps from bough to bough
But lazily; pauses; and settles now
Where once he stored his food.

One by one the flowers close,
Lily and dewy rose
Shutting their tender petals from the moon:
The grasshoppers are still; but not so soon
Are still the noisy crows.

The dormouse squats and eats
Choice little dainty bits
Beneath the spreading roots of a broad lime;
Nibbling his fill he stops from time to time
And listens where he sits.

From far the lowings come
Of cattle driven home:
From farther still the wind brings fitfully
The vast continual murmur of the sea,
Now loud, now almost dumb.

The gnats whirl in the air,
    The evening gnats; and there
The owl opes broad his eyes and wings to sail
For prey; the bat wakes; and the shell-less snail
    Comes forth, clammy and bare.

Hark! that's the nightingale,
    Telling the selfsame tale
Her song told when this ancient earth was young:
So echoes answered when her song was sung
    In the first wooded vale.

We call it love and pain
    The passion of her strain;
And yet we little understand or know:
Why should it not be rather joy that so
    Throbs in each throbbing vein?

In separate herds the deer
    Lie; here the bucks, and here
The does, and by its mother sleeps the fawn:
Through all the hours of night until the dawn
    They sleep, forgetting fear.

The hare sleeps where it lies,
    With wary half-closed eyes;
The cock has ceased to crow, the hen to cluck:
Only the fox is out, some heedless duck
    Or chicken to surprise.

Remote, each single star
    Comes out, till there they are

All shining brightly: how the dews fall damp!
While close at hand the glow-worm lights her lamp
    Or twinkles from afar.

    But evening now is done
    As much as if the sun
Day-giving had arisen in the East:
For night has come; and the great calm has ceased,
    The quiet sands have run.

Venus's Looking-Glass

I marked where lovely Venus and her court
    With song and dance and merry laugh went by;
    Weightless, their wingless feet seemed made to fly,
Bound from the ground and in mid air to sport.
Left far behind I heard the dolphins snort,
    Tracking their goddess with a wistful eye,
    Around whose head white doves rose, wheeling high
Or low, and cooed after their tender sort.
All this I saw in Spring. Thro' Summer heat
    I saw the lovely Queen of Love no more.
    But when flushed Autumn thro' the woodlands went
I spied sweet Venus walk amid the wheat:
    Whom seeing, every harvester gave o'er
    His toil, and laughed and hoped and was content.

A Peal of Bells

Strike the bells wantonly,
    Tinkle tinkle well;
Bring me wine, bring me flowers,
    Ring the silver bell.
All my lamps burn scented oil,
    Hung on laden orange trees,
Whose shadowed foliage is the foil
    To golden lamps and oranges.
Heap my golden plates with fruit,
    Golden fruit, fresh-plucked and ripe;
    Strike the bells and breathe the pipe;
Shut out showers from summer hours —
Silence that complaining lute —
    Shut out thinking, shut out pain,
    From hours that cannot come again.

Strike the bells solemnly,
    Ding dong deep:
My friend is passing to his bed,
    Fast asleep;
There's plaited linen round his head,
    While foremost go his feet, —
His feet that cannot carry him.
My feast's a show, my lights are dim;
    Be still, your music is not sweet, —
There is no music more for him:
    His lights are out, his feast is done;

His bowl that sparkled to the brim
Is drained, is broken, cannot hold;
My blood is chill, his blood is cold;
    His death is full, and mine begun.

Three Seasons

'A cup for hope!' she said,
In springtime ere the bloom was old:
The crimson wine was poor and cold
    By her mouth's richer red.

'A cup for love!' how low,
How soft the words; and all the while
Her blush was rippling with a smile
    Like summer after snow.

'A cup for memory!'
Cold cup that one must drain alone:
While autumn winds are up and moan
    Across the barren sea.

Hope, memory, love:
Hope for fair morn, and love for day,
And memory for the evening grey
    And solitary dove.

Beauty is Vain

While roses are so red,
    While lilies are so white,
Shall a woman exalt her face
    Because it gives delight?
She's not so sweet as a rose,
    A lily's straighter than she,
And if she were as red or white
    She'd be but one of three.

Whether she flush in love's summer
    Or in its winter grow pale,
Whether she flaunt her beauty
    Or hide it away in a veil,
Be she red or white,
    And stand she erect or bowed,
Time will win the race he runs with her
    And hide her away in a shroud.

Consider

Consider
The lilies of the field whose bloom is brief: —
We are as they;
Like them we fade away,
As doth a leaf.

Consider
The sparrows of the air of small account:
Our God doth view
Whether they fall or mount, —
He guards us too.

Consider
The lilies that do neither spin nor toil,
Yet are most fair: —
What profits all this care
And all this coil?

Consider
The birds that have no barn nor harvest-weeks;
God gives them food: —
Much more our Father seeks
To do us good.

On the Wing

Once in a dream (for once I dreamed of you)
    We stood together in an open field;
    Above our heads two swift-winged pigeons wheeled,
Sporting at ease and courting full in view.
When loftier still a broadening darkness flew,
    Down-swooping, and a ravenous hawk revealed;
    Too weak to fight, too fond to fly, they yield;
So farewell life and love and pleasures new.
Then, as their plumes fell fluttering to the ground,
    Their snow-white plumage flecked with crimson drops,
      I wept, and thought I turned towards you to weep:
    But you were gone; while rustling hedgerow tops
Bent in a wind which bore to me a sound
    Of far-off piteous bleat of lambs and sheep.

The Lowest Room

Like flowers sequestered from the sun
  And wind of summer, day by day
I dwindled paler, whilst my hair
   Showed the first tinge of grey.

'Oh, what is life, that we should live?
  Or what is death, that we must die?
A bursting bubble is our life:
   I also, what am I?'

'What is your grief? now tell me, sweet,
  That I may grieve,' my sister said;
And stayed a white embroidering hand
   And raised a golden head:

Her tresses showed a richer mass,
  Her eyes looked softer than my own,
Her figure had a statelier height,
   Her voice a tenderer tone.

'Some must be second and not first;
  All cannot be the first of all:
Is not this, too, but vanity?
   I stumble like to fall.

'So yesterday I read the acts
  Of Hector and each clangorous king
With wrathful great Æacides: –
   Old Homer leaves a sting.'

The comely face looked up again,
      The deft hand lingered on the thread
'Sweet, tell me what is Homer's sting,
      Old Homer's sting?' she said.

'He stirs my sluggish pulse like wine,
      He melts me like the wind of spice,
Strong as strong Ajax' red right hand,
      And grand like Juno's eyes.

'I cannot melt the sons of men,
      I cannot fire and tempest-toss: —
Besides, those days were golden days,
      Whilst these are days of dross.'

She laughed a feminine low laugh,
      Yet did not stay her dexterous hand:
'Now tell me of those days,' she said,
      'When time ran golden sand.'

'Then men were men of might and right,
      Sheer might, at least, and weighty swords;
Then men in open blood and fire
      Bore witness to their words,

'Crest-rearing kings with whistling spears;
      But if these shivered in the shock
They wrenched up hundred-rooted trees,
      Or hurled the effacing rock.

'Then hand to hand, then foot to foot,
      Stern to the death-grip grappling then,

Who ever thought of gunpowder
        Amongst these men of men?

'They knew whose hand struck home the death,
        They knew who broke but would not bend,
Could venerate an equal foe
        And scorn a laggard friend.

'Calm in the utmost stress of doom,
        Devout toward adverse powers above,
They hated with intenser hate
        And loved with fuller love.

'Then heavenly beauty could allay
        As heavenly beauty stirred the strife:
By them a slave was worshipped more
        Than is by us a wife.'

She laughed again, my sister laughed;
        Made answer o'er the laboured cloth:
'I rather would be one of us
        Than wife, or slave, or both.'

'Oh better then be slave or wife
        Than fritter now blank life away:
Then night had holiness of night,
        And day was sacred day.

'The princess laboured at her loom,
        Mistress and handmaiden alike;
Beneath their needles grew the field
        With warriors armed to strike.

'Or, look again, dim Dian's face
        Gleamed perfect thro' the attendant night:
Were such not better than those holes
        Amid that waste of white?

'A shame it is, our aimless life;
        I rather from my heart would feed
From silver dish in gilded stall
        With wheat and wine the steed —

'The faithful steed that bore my lord
        In safety thro' the hostile land,
The faithful steed that arched his neck
        To fondle with my hand.'

Her needle erred; a moment's pause,
        A moment's patience, all was well.
Then she: 'But just suppose the horse,
        Suppose the rider fell?

'Then captive in an alien house,
        Hungering on exile's bitter bread, —
They happy, they who won the lot
        Of sacrifice,' she said.

Speaking she faltered, while her look
        Showed forth her passion like a glass:
With hand suspended, kindling eye,
        Flushed cheek, how fair she was!

'Ah well, be those the days of dross;
        This, if you will, the age of gold:

Yet had those days a spark of warmth,
      While these are somewhat cold —

'Are somewhat mean and cold and slow,
      Are stunted from heroic growth:
We gain but little when we prove
      The worthlessness of both.'

'But life is in our hands,' she said;
      'In our own hands for gain or loss:
Shall not the Sevenfold Sacred Fire
      Suffice to purge our dross?

'Too short a century of dreams,
      One day of work sufficient length:
Why should not you, why should not I,
      Attain heroic strength?

'Our life is given us as a blank,
      Ourselves must make it blest or curst:
Who dooms me I shall only be
      The second, not the first?

'Learn from old Homer, if you will,
      Such wisdom as his books have said:
In one the acts of Ajax shine,
      In one of Diomed.

'Honoured all heroes whose high deeds
      Thro' life, thro' death, enlarge their span:
Only Achilles in his rage
      And sloth is less than man.'

'Achilles only less than man?
    He less than man who, half a god,
Discomfited all Greece with rest,
        Cowed Ilion with a nod?

'He offered vengeance, lifelong grief
    To one dear ghost, uncounted price:
Beasts, Trojans, adverse gods, himself,
        Heaped up the sacrifice.

'Self-immolated to his friend,
    Shrined in world's wonder, Homer's page,
Is this the man, the less than men
        Of this degenerate age?'

'Gross from his acorns, tusky boar
    Does memorable acts like his;
So for her snared offended young
        Bleeds the swart lioness.'

But here she paused; our eyes had met,
    And I was whitening with the jeer;
She rose: 'I went too far,' she said;
        Spoke low: 'Forgive me, dear.

'To me our days seem pleasant days,
    Our home a haven of pure content;
Forgive me if I said too much,
        So much more than I meant.

'Homer, tho' greater than his gods,
    With rough-hewn virtues was sufficed

And rough-hewn men: but what are such
        To us who learn of Christ?'

The much-moved pathos of her voice,
        Her almost tearful eyes, her cheek
Grown pale, confessed the strength of love
        Which only made her speak.

For mild she was, of few soft words,
        Most gentle, easy to be led,
Content to listen when I spoke,
        And reverence what I said:

I elder sister by six years;
        Not half so glad, or wise, or good:
Her words rebuked my secret self
        And shamed me where I stood.

She never guessed her words reproved
        A silent envy nursed within,
A selfish, souring discontent
        Pride-born, the devil's sin.

I smiled, half bitter, half in jest:
        'The wisest man of all the wise
Left for his summary of life
        'Vanity of vanities.'

'Beneath the sun there's nothing new:
        Men flow, men ebb, mankind flows on:
If I am wearied of my life,
        Why, so was Solomon.

'Vanity of vanities he preached
          Of all he found, of all he sought:
Vanity of vanities, the gist
          Of all the words he taught.

'This in the wisdom of the world,
          In Homer's page, in all, we find:
As the sea is not filled, so yearns
          Man's universal mind.

'This Homer felt, who gave his men
          With glory but a transient state:
His very Jove could not reverse
          Irrevocable fate.

'Uncertain all their lot save this –
          Who wins must lose, who lives must die:
All trodden out into the dark
          Alike, all vanity.'

She scarcely answered when I paused,
          But rather to herself said: 'One
Is here,' low-voiced and loving, 'Yea,
          Greater than Solomon.'

So both were silent, she and I:
          She laid her work aside, and went
Into the garden-walks, like spring,
          All gracious with content:

A little graver than her wont,
          Because her words had fretted me;

Not warbling quite her merriest tune
      Bird-like from tree to tree.

I chose a book to read and dream:
      Yet half the while with furtive eyes
Marked how she made her choice of flowers
      Intuitively wise,

And ranged them with instinctive taste
      Which all my books had failed to teach;
Fresh rose herself, and daintier
      Than blossom of the peach.

By birthright higher than myself,
      Tho' nestling of the selfsame nest:
No fault of hers, no fault of mine,
      But stubborn to digest.

I watched her, till my book unmarked
      Slid noiseless to the velvet floor;
Till all the opulent summer-world
      Looked poorer than before.

Just then her busy fingers ceased,
      Her fluttered colour went and came:
I knew whose step was on the walk,
      Whose voice would name her name.

* * * * *

Well, twenty years have passed since then:
      My sister now, a stately wife

Still fair, looks back in peace and sees
    The longer half of life –

The longer half of prosperous life,
    With little grief, or fear, or fret:
She, loved and loving long ago,
    Is loved and loving yet.

A husband honourable, brave,
    Is her main wealth in all the world:
And next to him one like herself,
    One daughter golden-curled;

Fair image of her own fair youth,
    As beautiful and as serene,
With almost such another love
    As her own love has been.

Yet, tho' of world-wide charity,
    And in her home most tender dove,
Her treasure and her heart are stored
    In the home-land of love.

She thrives, God's blessed husbandry;
    Most like a vine which full of fruit
Doth cling and lean and climb toward heaven,
    While earth still binds its root.

I sit and watch my sister's face:
    How little altered since the hours
When she, a kind, light-hearted girl,
    Gathered her garden flowers:

Her song just mellowed by regret
　　For having teased me with her talk;
Then all-forgetful as she heard
　　One step upon the walk.

While I? I sat alone and watched;
　　My lot in life, to live alone
In mine own world of interests,
　　Much felt, but little shown.

Not to be first: how hard to learn
　　That lifelong lesson of the past;
Line graven on line and stroke on stroke:
　　But, thank God, learned at last.

So now in patience I possess
　　My soul year after tedious year,
Content to take the lowest place,
　　The place assigned me here.

Yet sometimes, when I feel my strength
　　Most weak, and life most burdensome,
I lift mine eyes up to the hills
　　From whence my help shall come:

Yea, sometimes still I lift my heart
　　To the Archangelic trumpet-burst,
When all deep secrets shall be shown,
　　And many last be first.

What Would I Give?

What would I give for a heart of flesh to warm me thro',
Instead of this heart of stone ice-cold whatever I do;
Hard and cold and small, of all hearts the worst of all.

What would I give for words, if only words would come;
But now in its misery my spirit has fallen dumb:
O merry friends, go your way, I have never a word to say.

What would I give for tears, not smiles but scalding tears,
To wash the black mark clean, and to thaw the frost of years,
To wash the stain ingrain and to make me clean again.

What's in a Name?

Why has Spring one syllable less
Than any its fellow season?
There may be some other reason,
And I'm merely making a guess;
But surely it hoards such wealth
Of happiness, hope and health,
Sunshine and musical sound,
It may spare a foot from its name
Yet all the same
Superabound.

Soft-named Summer,
Most welcome comer,
Brings almost everything
Over which we dream or sing
Or sigh;
But then Summer wends its way,
Tomorrow, — today, —
Good-bye!

Autumn, — the slow name lingers,
While we likewise flag;
It silences many singers;
Its slow days drag,
Yet hasten at speed
To leave us in chilly need
For Winter to strip indeed.

In all-lack Winter,
Dull of sense and of sound,

We huddle and shiver
Beside our splinter
Of crackling pine,
Snow in sky and snow on ground.
Winter and cold
Can't last for ever!
Today, tomorrow, the sun will shine;
When we are old,
But some still are young,
Singing the song
Which others have sung,
Ringing the bells
Which others have rung, —
Even so!
We ourselves, who else?
We ourselves long
Long ago.

Echo

Come to me in the silence of the night;
    Come in the speaking silence of a dream;
Come with soft rounded cheeks and eyes as bright
    As sunlight on a stream;
      Come back in tears,
O memory, hope, love of finished years.

Oh dream how sweet, too sweet, too bitter sweet,
    Whose wakening should have been in Paradise,
Where souls brimful of love abide and meet;
    Where thirsting longing eyes
      Watch the slow door
That opening, letting in, lets out no more.

Yet come to me in dreams, that I may live
    My very life again tho' cold in death:
Come back to me in dreams, that I may give
    Pulse for pulse, breath for breath:
      Speak low, lean low,
As long ago, my love, how long ago.

After Death

The curtains were half drawn, the floor was swept
　　And strewn with rushes, rosemary and may
　　Lay thick upon the bed on which I lay,
Where thro' the lattice ivy-shadows crept.
He leaned above me, thinking that I slept
　　And could not hear him; but I heard him say:
　　'Poor child, poor child': and as he turned away
Came a deep silence, and I knew he wept.
He did not touch the shroud, or raise the fold
　　That hid my face, or take my hand in his,
　　　Or ruffle the smooth pillows for my head:
　　He did not love me living; but once dead
　　He pitied me; and very sweet it is
To know he still is warm tho' I am cold.

'The Master is Come, and Calleth for Thee'

Who calleth? – Thy Father calleth,
    Run, O Daughter, to wait on Him:
He Who chasteneth but for a season
    Trims thy lamp that it burn not dim.

Who calleth? – Thy Master calleth,
    Sit, Disciple, and learn of Him:
He Who teacheth wisdom of Angels
    Makes thee wise as the Cherubim,

Who calleth? – Thy Monarch calleth,
    Rise, O Subject, and follow Him:
He is stronger than Death or Devil,
    Fear not thou if the foe be grim.

Who calleth? – Thy Lord God calleth.
    Fall, O Creature, adoring Him:
He is jealous, thy God Almighty,
    Count not dear to thee life or limb.

Who calleth? – Thy Bridegroom calleth,
    Soar, O Bride, with the Seraphim:
He Who loves thee as no man loveth,
    Bids thee give up thy heart to Him.

May

I cannot tell you how it was;
But this I know: it came to pass
Upon a bright and breezy day
When May was young; ah, pleasant May!
As yet the poppies were not born
Between the blades of tender corn;
The last eggs had not hatched as yet,
Nor any bird foregone its mate.

I cannot tell you what it was;
But this I know: it did but pass.
It passed away with sunny May,
With all sweet things it passed away,
And left me old, and cold, and gray.

'No, Thank You, John'

I never said I loved you, John:
    Why will you tease me, day by day,
And wax a weariness to think upon
    With always 'do' and 'pray'?

You know I never loved you, John;
    No fault of mine made me your toast:
Why will you haunt me with a face as wan
    As shows an hour-old ghost?

I dare say Meg or Moll would take
    Pity upon you, if you'd ask:
And pray don't remain single for my sake
    Who can't perform that task.

I have no heart? – Perhaps I have not;
    But then you're mad to take offence
That I don't give you what I have not got:
    Use your own common sense.

Let bygones be bygones:
    Don't call me false, who owed not to be true:
I'd rather answer 'No' to fifty Johns
    Than answer 'Yes' to you.

Let's mar our pleasant days no more,
    Song-birds of passage, days of youth:
Catch at today, forget the days before:
    I'll wink at your untruth.

Let us strike hands as hearty friends;
    No more, no less: and friendship's good:
Only don't keep in view ulterior ends,
    And points not understood

In open treaty. Rise above
    Quibbles and shuffling off and on:
Here's friendship for you if you like; but love, —
    No, thank you, John.

Fata Morgana

A blue-eyed phantom far before
    Is laughing, leaping toward the sun;
Like lead I chase it evermore,
    I pant and run.

It breaks the sunlight bound on bound;
    Goes singing as it leaps along
To sheep-bells with a dreamy sound
    A dreamy song.

I laugh, it is so brisk and gay;
    It is so far before, I weep:
I hope I shall lie down some day,
    Lie down and sleep.

Memory

I.

I nursed it in my bosom while it lived,
    I hid it in my heart when it was dead;
In joy I sat alone, even so I grieved
        Alone and nothing said.

I shut the door to face the naked truth,
    I stood alone – I faced the truth alone,
Stripped bare of self-regard or forms or ruth
        Till first and last were shown.

I took the perfect balances and weighed;
    No shaking of my hand disturbed the poise;
Weighed, found it wanting: not a word I said,
        But silent made my choice.

None know the choice I made; I make it still.
    None know the choice I made and broke my heart,
Breaking mine idol: I have braced my will
        Once, chosen for once my part.

I broke it at a blow, I laid it cold,
    Crushed in my deep heart where it used to live.
My heart dies inch by inch; the time grows old,
        Grows old in which I grieve.

II.

I have a room whereinto no one enters
    Save I myself alone:
    There sits a blessed memory on a throne,
There my life centres;

While winter comes and goes — oh tedious comer! —
    And while its nip-wind blows;
    While bloom the bloodless lily and warm rose
Of lavish summer.

If any should force entrance he might see there
    One buried yet not dead,
    Before whose face I no more bow my head
Or bend my knee there;

But often in my worn life's autumn weather
    I watch there with clear eyes,
    And think how it will be in Paradise
When we're together.

Gone Forever

O happy rose-bud blooming
     Upon thy parent tree,
Nay, thou art too presuming;
For soon the earth entombing
     Thy faded charms shall be,
And the chill damp consuming.

O happy skylark springing
     Up to the broad blue sky,
Too fearless in thy winging,
Too gladsome in thy singing,
     Thou also soon shalt lie
Where no sweet notes are ringing.

And through life's shine and shower
     We shall have joy and pain;
But in the summer bower,
And at the morning hour,
     We still shall look in vain
For the same bird and flower.

A Royal Princess

I, a princess, king-descended, decked with jewels, gilded,
  drest,
Would rather be a peasant with her baby at her breast,
For all I shine so like the sun, and am purple like the West.

Two and two my guards behind, two and two before,
Two and two on either hand, they guard me evermore;
Me, poor dove, that must not coo, — eagle, that must not
  soar.

All my fountains cast up perfumes, all my gardens grow
Scented woods and foreign spices, with all flowers in blow
That are costly, out of season as the seasons go.

All my walls are lost in mirrors, whereupon I trace
Self to right hand, self to left hand, self in every place,
Self-same solitary figure, self-same seeking face.

Then I have an ivory chair high to sit upon,
Almost like my father's chair, which is an ivory throne;
There I sit uplift and upright, there I sit alone.

Alone by day, alone by night, alone days without end;
My father and my mother give me treasures, search and
  spend —
O my father! O my mother! have you ne'er a friend?

As I am a lofty princess, so my father is
A lofty king, accomplished in all kingly subtilties,
Holding in his strong right hand world-kingdoms' balances.

He has quarrelled with his neighbours, he has scourged
   his foes;
Vassal counts and princes follow where his pennon goes,
Long-descended valiant lords whom the vulture knows,

On whose track the vulture swoops, when they ride in state
To break the strength of armies and topple down the great:
Each of these my courteous servant, none of these my mate.

My father counting up his strength sets down with equal pen
So many head of cattle, head of horses, head of men;
These for slaughter, these for labor, with the how and when.

Some to work on roads, canals; some to man his ships;
Some to smart in mines beneath sharp overseers' whips;
Some to trap fur-beasts in lands where utmost winter nips.

Once it came into my heart and whelmed me like a flood,
That these too are men and women, human flesh and blood;
Men with hearts and men with souls, tho' trodden down
   like mud.

Our feasting was not glad that night, our music was not
   gay;
On my mother's graceful head I marked a thread of grey,
My father frowning at the fare seemed every dish to weigh.

I sat beside them sole princess in my exalted place,
My ladies and my gentlemen stood by me on the dais:
A mirror showed me I look old and haggard in the face;

It showed me that my ladies all are fair to gaze upon,

Plump, plenteous-haired, to every one love's secret lore is
    known,
They laugh by day, they sleep by night; ah me, what is a
    throne?

The singing men and women sang that night as usual,
The dancers danced in pairs and sets, but music had a fall,
A melancholy windy fall as at a funeral.

Amid the toss of torches to my chamber back we swept;
My ladies loosed my golden chain; meantime I could have
    wept
To think of some in galling chains whether they waked or
    slept.
I took my bath of scented milk, delicately waited on,
They burned sweet things for my delight, cedar and
    cinnamon,
They lit my shaded silver lamp and left me there alone.

A day went by, a week went by. One day I heard it said:
'Men are clamoring, women, children, clamoring to be fed;
Men like famished dogs are howling in the streets for bread.'

So two whispered by my door, not thinking I could hear,
Vulgar, naked truth, ungarnished for a royal ear;
Fit for cooping in the background, not to stalk so near.

But I strained my utmost sense to catch this truth, and mark:
'There are families out grazing like cattle in the park.'
'A pair of peasants must be saved even if we build an ark.'

A merry jest, a merry laugh, each strolled upon his way;

One was my page, a lad I reared and bore with day by day;
One was my youngest maid, as sweet and white as cream
in May.

Other footsteps followed softly with a weightier tramp;
Voices said: 'Picked soldiers have been summoned from
the camp,
To quell these base-born ruffians who make free to howl
and stamp.'
'Howl and stamp?' one answered: 'They made free to hurl
a stone
At the minister's state coach, well aimed and stoutly
thrown.'
'There's work, then, for the soldiers, for this rank crop
must be mown.'

'One I saw, a poor old fool with ashes on his head,
Whimpering because a girl had snatched his crust of bread:
Then he dropped; when some one raised him, it turned
out he was dead.'

'After us the deluge,' was retorted with a laugh:
'If bread's the staff of life, they must walk without a staff.'
'While I've a loaf they're welcome to my blessing and the
chaff.'

These passed. 'The king:'stand up. Said my father with a
smile:
'Daughter mine, your mother comes to sit with you awhile,
She's sad today, and who but you her sadness can beguile?'

He too left me. Shall I touch my harp now while I wait

(I hear them doubling guard below before our palace
    gate),
Or shall I work the last gold stitch into my veil of state;

Or shall my woman stand and read some unimpassioned
    scene,
There's music of a lulling sort in words that pause between;
Or shall she merely fan me while I wait here for the queen?

Again I caught my father's voice in sharp word of
    command:
'Charge!' a clash of steel: 'Charge again, the rebels stand.
Smite and spare not, hand to hand; smite and spare not,
    hand to hand.'

There swelled a tumult at the gate, high voices waxing
    higher;
A flash of red reflected light lit the cathedral spire;
I heard a cry for faggots, then I heard a yell for fire.

'Sit and roast there with your meat, sit and bake there
    with your bread,
You who sat to see us starve,' one shrieking woman said:
'Sit on your throne and roast with your crown upon your
    head.'

Nay, this thing will I do, while my mother tarrieth,
I will take my fine spun gold, but not to sew therewith,
I will take my gold and gems, and rainbow fan and
    wreath;

With a ransom in my lap, a king's ransom in my hand,

I will go down to this people, will stand face to face, will
  stand
Where they curse king, queen, and princess of this cursed
  land.
They shall take all to buy them bread, take all I have to give;
I, if I perish, perish; they today shall eat and live;
I, if I perish, perish; that's the goal I half conceive:

Once to speak before the world, rend bare my heart and
  show
The lesson I have learned, which is death, is life, to know.
I, if I perish, perish; in the name of God I go.

Vanity of Vanities

Ah, woe is me for pleasure that is vain,
    Ah, woe is me for glory that is past:
    Pleasure that bringeth sorrow at the last,
Glory that at the last bringeth no gain!
So saith the sinking heart; and so again
    It shall say till the mighty angel-blast
    Is blown, making the sun and moon aghast,
And showering down the stars like sudden rain.
And evermore men shall go fearfully,
    Bending beneath their weight of heaviness;
And ancient men shall lie down wearily,
    And strong men shall rise up in weariness;
Yea, even the young shall answer sighingly,
    Saying one to another: How vain it is!

A Portrait

I.

She gave up beauty in her tender youth,
    Gave all her hope and joy and pleasant ways;
    She covered up her eyes lest they should gaze
On vanity, and chose the bitter truth.
Harsh towards herself, towards others full of ruth,
    Servant of servants, little known to praise,
    Long prayers and fasts trenched on her nights and
        days:
She schooled herself to sights and sounds uncouth,
That with the poor and stricken she might make
    A home, until the least of all sufficed
Her wants; her own self learned she to forsake,
Counting all earthly gain but hurt and loss.
So with calm will she chose and bore the cross,
    And hated all for love of Jesus Christ.

II.

They knelt in silent anguish by her bed,
    And could not weep; but calmly there she lay.
    All pain had left her; and the sun's last ray
Shone through upon her, warming into red
The shady curtains. In her heart she said:
    'Heaven opens; I leave these and go away:
    The Bridegroom calls, – shall the Bride seek to stay?'
Then low upon her breast she bowed her head.
O lily-flower, O gem of priceless worth,
    O dove with patient voice and patient eyes,

O fruitful vine amid a land of dearth,
    O maid replete with loving purities,
Thou bowedst down thy head with friends on earth
    To raise it with the saints in Paradise.

Child's Talk in April

I wish you were a pleasant wren,
    And I your small accepted mate;
How we'd look down on toilsome men!
    We'd rise and go to bed at eight
    Or it may be not quite so late.

Then you should see the nest I'd build,
    The wondrous nest for you and me;
The outside rough, perhaps, but filled
    With wool and down: ah, you should see
    The cosy nest that it would be.

We'd have our change of hope and fear,
    Small quarrels, reconcilements sweet:
I'd perch by you to chirp and cheer,
    Or hop about on active feet
    And fetch you dainty bits to eat.

We'd be so happy by the day,
    So safe and happy thro' the night,
We both should feel, and I should say,
    It's all one season of delight,
And we'll make merry whilst we may.

Perhaps some day there'd be an egg
    When spring had blossomed from the snow:
I'd stand triumphant on one leg;
    Like chanticleer I'd almost crow
    To let our little neighbours know.

Next you should sit and I would sing
Thro' lengthening days of sunny spring:
       Till, if you wearied of the task,
I'd sit; and you should spread your wing
       From bough to bough; I'd sit and bask.

Fancy the breaking of the shell,
       The chirp, the chickens wet and bare,
The untried proud paternal swell;
       And you with housewife-matron air
       Enacting choicer bills of fare.

Fancy the embryo coats of down,
       The gradual feathers soft and sleek;
Till clothed and strong from tail to crown,
       With virgin warblings in their beak,
       They too go forth to soar and seek.

So would it last an April thro'
And early summer fresh with dew:
       Then should we part and live as twain,
Love-time would bring me back to you
       And build our happy nest again.

Bird or Beast?

Did any bird come flying
    After Adam and Eve,
When the door was shut against them
    And they sat down to grieve?

I think not Eve's peacock
    Splendid to see,
And I think not Adam's eagle;
    But a dove may be.

Did any beast come pushing
    Thro' the thorny hedge
Into the thorny, thistly world
    Out from Eden's edge?

I think not a lion,
    Tho' his strength is such;
But an innocent loving lamb
    May have done as much.

If the dove preached from her bough
    And the lamb from his sod,
The lamb and the dove
    Were preachers sent from God.

The Lambs of Grasmere, 1860

The upland flocks grew starved and thinned:
    Their shepherds scarce could feed the lambs
Whose milkless mothers butted them,
    Or who were orphaned of their dams.
The lambs athirst for mother's milk
    Filled all the place with piteous sounds:
Their mothers' bones made white for miles
    The pastureless wet pasture grounds.

Day after day, night after night,
    From lamb to lamb the shepherds went,
With teapots for the bleating mouths
    Instead of nature's nourishment.
The little shivering gaping things
    Soon knew the step that brought them aid,
And fondled the protecting hand,
    And rubbed it with a woolly head.

Then, as the days waxed on to weeks,
    It was a pretty sight to see
These lambs with frisky heads and tails
    Skipping and leaping on the lea,
Bleating in tender, trustful tones,
    Resting on rocky crag or mound,
And following the beloved feet
    That once had sought for them and found.

These very shepherds of their flocks,
    These loving lambs so meek to please,
Are worthy of recording words

And honour in their due degrees:
So I might live a hundred years,
And roam from strand to foreign strand,
Yet not forget this flooded spring
And scarce-saved lambs of Westmoreland.

Winter Rain

Every valley drinks,
    Every dell and hollow:
Where the kind rain sinks and sinks,
    Green of Spring will follow.

Yet a lapse of weeks
    Buds will burst their edges,
Strip their wool-coats, glue-coats, streaks,
    In the woods and hedges;

Weave a bower of love
    For birds to meet each other,
Weave a canopy above
    Nest and egg and mother.

But for fattening rain
    We should have no flowers,
Never a bud or leaf again
    But for soaking showers;

Never a mated bird
    In the rocking tree-tops,
Never indeed a flock or herd
    To graze upon the lea-crops.

Lambs so woolly white,
    Sheep the sun-bright leas on,
They could have no grass to bite
    But for rain in season.

We should find no moss
        In the shadiest places,
Find no waving meadow grass
        Pied with broad-eyed daisies;

But miles of barren sand,
        With never a son or daughter,
Not a lily on the land,
        Or lily on the water.

The First Spring Day

I wonder if the sap is stirring yet,
If wintry birds are dreaming of a mate,
If frozen snowdrops feel as yet the sun
And crocus fires are kindling one by one:
    Sing, robin, sing!
I still am sore in doubt concerning Spring.

I wonder if the springtide of this year
Will bring another Spring both lost and dear;
If heart and spirit will find out their Spring,
Or if the world alone will bud and sing:
    Sing, hope, to me!
Sweet notes, my hope, soft notes for memory.

The sap will surely quicken soon or late,
The tardiest bird will twitter to a mate;
So Spring must dawn again with warmth and bloom,
Or in this world, or in the world to come:
    Sing, voice of Spring!
Till I too blossom and rejoice and sing.

The Queen of Hearts

How comes it, Flora, that, whenever we
Play cards together, you invariably,
    However the pack parts,
    Still hold the Queen of Hearts?

I've scanned you with a scrutinizing gaze,
Resolved to fathom these your secret ways:
    But, sift them as I will,
    Your ways are secret still.

I cut and shuffle; shuffle, cut, again;
But all my cutting, shuffling, proves in vain:
    Vain hope, vain forethought, too;
    That Queen still falls to you.

I dropped her once, prepense; but, ere the deal
Was dealt, your instinct seemed her loss to feel:
    'There should be one card more,'
    You said, and searched the floor.

I cheated once: I made a private notch
In Heart-Queen's back, and kept a lynx-eyed watch;
    Yet such another back
    Deceived me in the pack:

The Queen of Clubs assumed by arts unknown
An imitative dint that seemed my own;
    This notch, not of my doing,
    Misled me to my ruin.

It baffles me to puzzle out the clue,
Which must be skill, or craft, or luck in you:
    Unless, indeed, it be
    Natural affinity.

Cousin Kate

I was a cottage maiden
Hardened by sun and air,
Contented with my cottage mates,
Not mindful I was fair.
Why did a great lord find me out,
And praise my flaxen hair?
Why did a great lord find me out
To fill my heart with care?

He lured me to his palace home —
Woe's me for joy thereof —
To lead a shameless shameful life,
His plaything and his love.
He wore me like a silken knot,
He changed me like a glove;
So now I moan, an unclean thing,
Who might have been a dove.

O Lady Kate, my cousin Kate,
You grew more fair than I:
He saw you at your father's gate,
Chose you, and cast me by.
He watched your steps along the lane,
Your work among the rye;
He lifted you from mean estate
To sit with him on high.

Because you were so good and pure
He bound you with his ring:
The neighbours call you good and pure,

Call me an outcast thing.
Even so I sit and howl in dust,
You sit in gold and sing:
Now which of us has tenderer heart?
You had the stronger wing.

O cousin Kate, my love was true,
Your love was writ in sand:
If he had fooled not me but you,
If you stood where I stand,
He'd not have won me with his love
Nor bought me with his land;
I would have spit into his face
And not have taken his hand.

Yet I've a gift you have not got,
And seem not like to get:
For all your clothes and wedding-ring
I've little doubt you fret.
My fair-haired son, my shame, my pride,
Cling closer, closer yet:
Your father would give lands for one
To wear his coronet.

A Bird's-Eye View

'Croak, croak, croak,'
Thus the Raven spoke,
Perched on his crooked tree
As hoarse as hoarse could be.
Shun him and fear him,
Lest the Bridegroom hear him;
Scout him and rout him
With his ominous eye about him.

Yet, 'Croak, croak, croak,'
Still tolled from the oak;
From that fatal black bird,
Whether heard or unheard:
'O ship upon the high seas,
Freighted with lives and spices,
Sink, O ship,' croaked the Raven:
'Let the Bride mount to heaven.'

In a far foreign land
Upon the wave-edged sand,
Some friends gaze wistfully
Across the glittering sea.
'If we could clasp our sister,'
Three say, 'now we have missed her!'
'If we could kiss our daughter!'
Two sigh across the water.

Oh, the ship sails fast,
With silken flags at the mast,
And the home-wind blows soft;

But a Raven sits aloft,
Chuckling and choking,
Croaking, croaking, croaking: —
Let the beacon-fire blaze higher;
Bridegroom, watch; the Bride draws nigher.

On a sloped sandy beach,
Which the spring-tide billows reach,
Stand a watchful throng
Who have hoped and waited long:
'Fie on this ship, that tarries
With the priceless freight it carries.
The time seems long and longer:
O languid wind, wax stronger'; —

Whilst the Raven perched at ease
Still croaks and does not cease,
One monotonous note
Tolled from his iron throat:
'No father, no mother,
But I have a sable brother:
He sees where ocean flows to,
And he knows what he knows, too.'

A day and a night
They kept watch worn and white;
A night and a day
For the swift ship on its way:
For the Bride and her maidens,
 — Clear chimes the bridal cadence —
For the tall ship that never
Hove in sight forever.

On either shore, some
Stand in grief loud or dumb
As the dreadful dread
Grows certain tho' unsaid.
For laughter there is weeping,
And waking instead of sleeping,
And a desperate sorrow
Morrow after morrow.

Oh, who knows the truth,
How she perished in her youth,
And like a queen went down
Pale in her royal crown?
How she went up to glory
From the sea-foam chill and hoary,
From the sea-depth black and riven
To the calm that is in Heaven?

They went down, all the crew,
The silks and spices too,
The great ones and the small,
One and all, one and all.
Was it thro' stress of weather,
Quicksands, rocks, or all together?
Only the Raven knows this,
And he will not disclose this. —

After a day and a year
The bridal bells chime clear;
After a year and a day
The Bridegroom is brave and gay:
Love is sound, faith is rotten;

The old Bride is forgotten: —
Two ominous Ravens only
Remember, black and lonely.

A Better Resurrection

I have no wit, no words, no tears;
    My heart within me like a stone
Is numbed too much for hopes or fears;
    Look right, look left, I dwell alone;
I lift mine eyes, but dimmed with grief
    No everlasting hills I see;
My life is in the falling leaf:
    O Jesus, quicken me!

My life is like a faded leaf,
    My harvest dwindled to a husk;
Truly my life is void and brief
    And tedious in the barren dusk;
My life is like a frozen thing,
    No bud nor greenness can I see:
Yet rise it shall, – the sap of Spring;
    O Jesus, rise in me!

My life is like a broken bowl,
    A broken bowl that cannot hold
One drop of water for my soul
    Or cordial in the searching cold;
Cast in the fire the perished thing,
    Melt and remould it, till it be
A royal cup for Him my King:
    O Jesus, drink of me!

Fluttered Wings

The splendour of the kindling day,
    The splendour of the setting sun,
These move my soul to wend its way,
    And have done
With all we grasp and toil amongst and say.

The paling roses of a cloud,
    The fading bow that arches space,
These woo my fancy toward my shroud;
    Toward the place
Of faces veiled, and heads discrowned and bowed.

The nation of the awful stars,
    The wandering star whose blaze is brief,
These make me beat against the bars
    Of my grief;
My tedious grief, twin to the life it mars.

O fretted heart tossed to and fro,
    So fain to flee, so fain to rest!
All glories that are high or low,
    East or west,
Grow dim to thee who art so fain to go.

A Hope Carol

A night was near, a day was near;
    Between a day and night
I heard sweet voices calling clear,
    Calling me:
I heard a whirr of wing on wing,
    But could not see the sight;
I long to see my birds that sing,
    I long to see.

Below the stars, beyond the moon,
    Between the night and day,
I heard a rising falling tune
    Calling me:
I long to see the pipes and strings
    Whereon such minstrels play;
I long to see each face that sings,
    I long to see.

Today or may be not today,
    Tonight or not tonight;
All voices that command or pray,
    Calling me,
Shall kindle in my soul such fire,
    And in my eyes such light,
That I shall see that heart's desire
    I long to see.

The Three Enemies

THE FLESH
'Sweet, thou art pale.'
    'More pale to see,
Christ hung upon the cruel tree
And bore His Father's wrath for me.'

'Sweet, thou art sad.'
    'Beneath a rod
More heavy, Christ for my sake trod
The winepress of the wrath of God.'

'Sweet, thou art weary.'
    'Not so Christ:
Whose mighty love of me sufficed
For Strength, Salvation, Eucharist.'

'Sweet, thou art footsore.'
    'If I bleed,
His feet have bled: yea, in my need
His Heart once bled for mine indeed.'

THE WORLD
'Sweet, thou art young.'
    'So He was young
Who for my sake in silence hung
Upon the Cross with Passion wrung.'

'Look, thou art fair.'
    'He was more fair
Than men, Who deigned for me
  to wear
A visage marred beyond compare.'

'And thou hast riches.'
    'Daily bread:
All else is His; Who living, dead,
For me lacked where to lay
  His Head.'

'And life is sweet.'
    'It was not so
To Him, Whose Cup did overflow
With mine unutterable woe.'

THE DEVIL
'Thou drinkest deep.'
    'When Christ would sup
He drained the dregs from out
  my cup:
So how should I be lifted up?'

'Thou shalt win Glory.'
    'In the skies,
Lord Jesus, cover up mine eyes
Lest they should look on vanities.'

'Thou shalt have Knowledge.'
    'Helpless dust,
In Thee, O Lord, I put my trust:
Answer Thou for me, Wise
    and Just.'
'And Might.'
    'Get thee behind me. Lord,
Who hast redeemed and not abhorred
My soul, Oh keep it by Thy Word.'

A Testimony

I said of laughter: it is vain.
    Of mirth I said: what profits it?
    Therefore I found a book, and writ
Therein how ease and also pain,
How health and sickness, every one
Is vanity beneath the sun.

Man walks in a vain shadow; he
    Disquieteth himself in vain.
    The things that were shall be again.
The rivers do not fill the sea,
But turn back to their secret source;
The winds too turn upon their course.

Our treasures moth and rust corrupt,
    Or thieves break thro' and steal, or they
    Make themselves wings and fly away.
One man made merry as he supped,
Nor guessed how when that night grew dim
His soul would be required of him.

We build our houses on the sand,
    Comely withoutside and within;
    But when the winds and rains begin
To beat on them, they cannot stand;
They perish, quickly overthrown,
Loose from the very basement stone.

All things are vanity, I said,
    Yea, vanity of vanities.

The rich man dies; and the poor dies;
The worm feeds sweetly on the dead.
Whate'er thou lackest, keep this trust:
All in the end shall have but dust:

The one inheritance, which best
    And worst alike shall find and share:
    The wicked cease from troubling there,
And there the weary be at rest;
There all the wisdom of the wise
Is vanity of vanities.

Man flourishes as a green leaf,
    And as a leaf doth pass away;
    Or, as a shade that cannot stay
And leaves no track, his course is brief:
Yet man doth hope and fear and plan
Till he is dead: – Oh foolish man!

Our eyes cannot be satisfied
    With seeing, nor our ears be filled
    With hearing: yet we plant and build
And buy and make our borders wide;
We gather wealth, we gather care,
But know not who shall be our heir.

Why should we hasten to arise
    So early, and so late take rest?
    Our labour is not good; our best
Hopes fade; our heart is stayed on lies:
Verily, we sow wind; and we
Shall reap the whirlwind, verily.

He who hath little shall not lack;
　　He who hath plenty shall decay:
　　Our fathers went; we pass away;
Our children follow on our track:
So generations fail, and so
They are renewed and come and go.

The earth is fattened with our dead;
　　She swallows more and doth not cease:
　　Therefore her wine and oil increase
And her sheaves are not numberèd;
Therefore her plants are green, and all
Her pleasant trees lusty and tall.

Therefore the maidens cease to sing,
　　And the young men are very sad;
　　Therefore the sowing is not glad,
And mournful is the harvesting.
Of high and low, of great and small,
Vanity is the lot of all.

A King dwelt in Jerusalem;
　　He was the wisest man on earth;
　　He had all riches from his birth,
And pleasures till he tired of them;
Then, having tested all things, he
Witnessed that all are vanity.

Patience of Hope

The flowers that bloom in sun and shade
    And glitter in the dew,
      The flowers must fade.
The birds that build their nest and sing
    When lovely spring is new,
      Must soon take wing.

The sun that rises in his strength
    To wake and warm the world,
      Must set at length.
The sea that overflows the shore
    With billows frothed and curled,
      Must ebb once more.

All come and go, all wax and wane,
    O Lord, save only Thou
      Who dost remain
The Same to all eternity.
    All things which fail us now
      We trust to Thee.

A Fisher-Wife

The soonest mended, nothing said;
    And help may rise from east or west;
But my two hands are lumps of lead,
    My heart sits leaden in my breast.

O north wind swoop not from the north,
    O south wind linger in the south,
Oh come not raving raging forth,
    To bring my heart into my mouth;

For I've a husband out at sea,
    Afloat on feeble planks of wood;
He does not know what fear may be;
    I would have told him if I could.

I would have locked him in my arms,
    I would have hid him in my heart;
For oh! the waves are fraught with harms,
    And he and I so far apart.

Shall I Forget?

Shall I forget on this side of the grave?
I promise nothing: you must wait and see
    Patient and brave.
(O my soul, watch with him and he with me.)

Shall I forget in peace of Paradise?
I promise nothing: follow, friend, and see
    Faithful and wise.
(O my soul, lead the way he walks with me.)

Index of First Lines